Government-Opposition in Southern European Countries during the Economic Crisis

The international economic crisis has hit Europe, especially its 'periphery', remarkably hard, and has had deep consequences at economic and political levels. Since its onset, parties in parliament (especially those in opposition) have found themselves faced with a dilemma: choosing between the need to cooperate with the government in order to overcome the crisis and the opportunity provided by a weakened government to stress their adversarial position, so as to be more easily re-elected and possibly get into power. What have they decided to do? This is a crucial question, for which there is no easy or intuitive answer. The present volume introduces a collection of works exploring this dilemma in southern European countries, by examining the opposition behaviour in Greece, Italy, Portugal and Spain, and in the European Parliament. In so doing, we shall try to understand not only what kind of impact the crisis has had on the level of consensus in parliament in the four countries mentioned, but also whether differences are observable across cases.

This book was originally published as a special issue of *The Journal of Legislative Studies*.

Elisabetta De Giorgi is a Postdoctoral Fellow at the FCSH-NOVA University of Lisbon. Her main research interests are parliaments from a comparative perspective, in particular, parliamentary opposition and the law-making process. She has published several articles in national and international journals – in *Acta Politica*, *The Journal of Legislative Studies*, *Journal of Modern Italian Studies*, *Italian Political Science Review*, *South European Society and Politics*, among others, and book chapters.

Catherine Moury is Assistant Professor at the FCSH-NOVA University of Lisbon. Her research focuses on institutional change in the EU and comparative policy-making. She has published in journals such as the *European Journal of Public Policy*, *West European Politics* and *Party Politics*. She is the author of *Coalition Government and Party Mandate: How coalition agreements constrain ministerial action* (Routledge, 2013) and *Changing Rules of Delegation: A contest for power in comitology* (with A. Héritier, C. Bischoff, C-F. Bergström, Oxford University Press, 2013).

Library of Legislative Studies
Edited by Lord Philip Norton of Louth, University of Hull, UK.

Government-Opposition in Southern European Countries during the Economic Crisis

Great recession, great cooperation?

Edited by
**Elisabetta De Giorgi and
Catherine Moury**

LONDON AND NEW YORK

First published 2016
by Routledge
2 Park Square, Milton Park, Abingdon, Oxon, OX14 4RN, UK

and by Routledge
711 Third Avenue, New York, NY 10017, USA

Routledge is an imprint of the Taylor & Francis Group, an informa business

British Library Cataloguing in Publication Data
A catalogue record for this book is available from the British Library

ISBN 13: 978-0-415-81752-3

Typeset in Times
by RefineCatch Limited, Bungay, Suffolk

Publisher's Note
The publisher accepts responsibility for any inconsistencies that may have arisen during the
conversion of this book from journal articles to book chapters, namely the possible inclusion of
journal terminology.

Disclaimer
Every effort has been made to contact copyright holders for their permission to reprint material
in this book. The publishers would be grateful to hear from any copyright holder who is not here
acknowledged and will undertake to rectify any errors or omissions in future editions of this book.

Contents

Citation Information

The chapters in this book were originally published in *The Journal of Legislative Studies*, volume 21, issue 1 (March 2015). When citing this material, please use the original page numbering for each article, as follows:

Chapter 1
Introduction: Conflict and Consensus in Parliament during the Economic Crisis
Catherine Moury and Elisabetta De Giorgi
The Journal of Legislative Studies, volume 21, issue 1 (March 2015) pp. 1–13

Chapter 2
Government–Opposition Dynamics during the Economic Crisis in Greece
Kostas Gemenis and Roula Nezi
The Journal of Legislative Studies, volume 21, issue 1 (March 2015) pp. 14–34

Chapter 3
From a Technocratic Solution to a Fragile Grand Coalition*: The Impact of the Economic Crisis on Parliamentary Government in Italy*
Francesco Marangoni and Luca Verzichelli
The Journal of Legislative Studies, volume 21, issue 1 (March 2015) pp. 35–53

Chapter 4
Incumbents, Opposition and International Lenders: Governing Portugal in Times of Crisis
Elisabetta De Giorgi, Catherine Moury and João Pedro Ruivo
The Journal of Legislative Studies, volume 21, issue 1 (March 2015) pp. 54–74

Chapter 5
Government–Opposition Dynamics in Spain under the Pressure of Economic Collapse and the Debt Crisis
Anna M. Palau, Luz Muñoz Márquez and Laura Chaqués-Bonafont
The Journal of Legislative Studies, volume 21, issue 1 (March 2015) pp. 75–95

Chapter 6

An Emerging Divide? Assessing the Impact of the Euro Crisis on the Voting Alignments of the European Parliament
Stefano Braghiroli
The Journal of Legislative Studies, volume 21, issue 1 (March 2015) pp. 96–114

Chapter 7

Conclusions: Great Recession, Great Cooperation?
Elisabetta De Giorgi and Catherine Moury
The Journal of Legislative Studies, volume 21, issue 1 (March 2015) pp. 115–120

For any permission-related enquiries please visit:
http://www.tandfonline.com/page/help/permissions

Notes on Contributors

Laura Chaqués-Bonafont is ICREA Professor of Political Science at the University of Barcelona and Research Fellow at the Institut Barcelona d'Estudis Internacionals (IBEI). She is the Director of the Spanish Policy Agendas Project (www.ub.edu/spanishpolicyagendas). She is the author of *Policy Dynamics in Spain* (2015 with A. M. Palau and F. R. Baumgartner), *Redes de Políticas Públicas* (2004) and *Estructura y Política farmacéutica* (2002) and several articles in journals such as *Political Communication, Comparative Political Studies, Journal of Public Policy* and *West European Politics*. Her main research interests are the analysis of agenda dynamics in comparative perspective, with special reference to the impact of the media, and interest groups. In 2015 she was awarded with the ICREA academia prize.

Stefano Braghiroli is a Lecturer at the Institute of Government and Politics (University of Tartu) and research affiliate to the Centre for EU-Russia Studies (CEURUS). He received his PhD from the University of Siena in 2010. His main research interests include party politics in the European Parliament, EU-Russia relations, electoral politics in Central and Eastern Europe and Turkey, and e-politics. His most recent publications include articles in *Southeast European and Black Sea Studies, Religion, State and Society*, and the *Journal of Contemporary European Studies* and various book chapters in publications with highly renowned publishers.

Elisabetta De Giorgi is a Postdoctoral Fellow at the FCSH-NOVA University of Lisbon. Her main research interests are parliaments from a comparative perspective, in particular, parliamentary opposition and the law-making process. She has published several articles in national and international journals including *Acta Politica, The Journal of Legislative Studies, Journal of Modern Italian Studies, Italian Political Science Review, South European Society and Politics*, among others, and book chapters.

Kostas Gemenis is Assistant Professor of Research Methods in the Department of Public Administration, University of Twente. His research interests include comparative European politics with a focus on the policy positions of political parties, conceptualization and measurement, and Greek party politics. His work has been published in journals such as *Electoral Studies*, *Party Politics*, *Comparative European Politics* and *European Political Science Review*.

Francesco Marangoni has a PhD in Comparative and European Politics from the University of Siena. He is research affiliate at both the Centre for the Analysis of Public Policy (CAPP) of the University of Bologna and the Centre for the Study of Political Change (CIRCaP) of the University of Siena, where he collaborates with the Observatory on Institutional Change. His main research interests include legislative behaviour, coalition governments and political elites. He has recently co-edited *The Challenge of Coalition Government. The Italian case* (Routledge, 2014).

Catherine Moury is Assistant Professor at the FCSH-NOVA University of Lisbon. Her research focuses on institutional change in the European Union and on comparative policy-making. She has published in journals such as *European Journal of Public Policy*, *West European Politics* and *Party Politics*. She is the author of *Coalition Government and Party Mandate: How coalition agreements constrain ministerial action* (Routledge, 2013) and *Changing Rules of Delegation: A contest for power in comitology* (with A. Héritier, C. Bischoff, C-F. Bergström, Oxford University Press, 2013).

Luz Muñoz Márquez is Assistant Professor in the Department of Constitutional Law and Political Science at the University of Barcelona. She is also a member of the Spanish Policy Agendas Project. She finished her PhD in Political Science at the University of Barcelona in 2012, she has been Visiting Researcher at the School of Geography, Politics and Sociology, University of Newcastle (2013), at the Faculty of Law, Universidad Iberoamericana (2013) and at the Center for American Politics and Public Policy, University of Washington (2009). Her current research focuses on interest groups politics, with special interest on NGOs and advocacy groups. Other topics are agenda setting and government–opposition dynamics.

Roula Nezi is a Postdoctoral Fellow at the Chair for Political Science, Policy Analysis and Political Theory, in the Department of Politics and Public Administration, University of Konstanz. Her research interests include voting behaviour, left-right ideology, party competition and political methodology. Her work has included participation in a transnational project on European citizenship, and she is currently involved in an inquiry about political extremism in the economic crisis. Her work has been published in *Electoral Studies*, *Europe-Asia Studies* and *South European Society and Politics*.

Anna M. Palau is Assistant Professor in the Department of Constitutional Law and Political Science at the University of Barcelona and a member of the Spanish Policy Agendas Project. Her research focuses on the analysis of policy dynamics, Europeanisation, media and public opinion and government–opposition dynamics. She is co-author of the book *Policy Dynamics in Spain* (2015, with Laura Chaqués-Bonafont and F. R. Baumgartner) and has published articles in *Comparative Political Studies*, *West European Politics*, *Journal of Public Policy* and *The Journal of Legislative Studies*, among others.

João Pedro Ruivo holds an MSc in Comparative and European Politics from the University of Siena (2005) and is currently a PhD candidate in Political Science at the NOVA University of Lisbon. His co-authored papers on elite attitudes and behaviour, and on Portuguese political science as a discipline have been published in *European Political Science*, *The Journal of Legislative Studies*, and *South European Society and Politics*. Professionally, he worked for the Portuguese Government as Knowledge Society Policy Officer (2001–2004) and Executive Coordinator of a nationwide action plan of ICT diffusion in K12 public schools (2007–2010). He has been teaching Political Institutions to Chinese mobility students at the NOVA since 2012.

Luca Verzichelli is Professor of Italian Politics and Public Policy Analysis at the University of Siena. He has been Chief Editor of the *Italian Journal of Political Science*. He is currently a member of the Editorial board of *Politica*, *South European Society and Politics* and *The Journal of Legislative Studies*. His research interests are concentrated on political institutions and political elites. Among his recent publications: *Political Institutions in Italy* (Oxford University Press, 2007, with Maurizio Cotta), *The Europe of Elites* (Oxford University Press, 2007, edited with H. Best and G. Lengyel) and *Manuale di Scienza Politica* (Il Mulino, with Giliberto Capano, Simona Piattoni and Francesco Raniolo).

Introduction: Conflict and Consensus in Parliament during the Economic Crisis

CATHERINE MOURY and ELISABETTA DE GIORGI

Since the onset of the economic crisis, parties in parliament (especially those in opposition) have found themselves faced with a dilemma: choosing between the need to cooperate with the government in order to overcome the crisis and the opportunity provided by a weakened government to stress their adversarial position so as to be more easily re-elected and possibly get into power. What have they decided to do? The present contribution introduces a collection of works exploring this dilemma in southern European countries, by examining the opposition behaviour in Greece, Italy, Portugal and Spain; and in the European Parliament.

Introduction

The international financial crisis has hit Europe, especially its 'periphery', remarkably hard, and has had deep consequences at the economic and political levels. A series of works have explored and explained the public policy reforms undertaken;[1] others have examined the electoral costs of such a difficult situation.[2] An important aspect that has not been addressed in the literature so far is the impact of the crisis on the level of consensus in parliament. This is striking, given its importance in empirical terms: the lack of cooperation between parliamentary party groups and the government has significant consequences in terms of bills' passage and legitimacy, and even in terms of government survival. Theoretically, the question is also interesting: parties in parliament (especially those in opposition) have found themselves faced with a dilemma: choosing between the need to cooperate with the government in order to overcome the crisis and the opportunity provided by a weakened government to stress their adversarial position so as to be more easily re-elected and possibly get into power. What have they decided to do? This is a crucial question, for which there is no easy or intuitive answer.

The present contribution introduces a collection of works exploring this dilemma in southern European countries, by examining the opposition behaviour in Greece, Italy, Portugal and Spain. In so doing, we shall try to understand not only what kind of impact the crisis has had on the level of consensus in parliament in the four countries mentioned, but also whether differences are observable across cases. We choose also to focus on the European Parliament (EP). Although there is not a clear government–opposition division across the EP, studies have shown that MPs behave differently when their national party is 'in government' in the EU Council and Commission (Hix, Noury, & Roland, 2006). This is particularly true for very relevant legislation or political deals that Council or Commission leaders pressure *their* members of the EP (MEPs) to support. Thus, like their counterparts in national parliaments, MEPs have found themselves under two contrasting pressures induced by the crisis: a pressure for cohesion, caused by the same sense of responsibility and state of emergency felt by the national opposition parties; and a pressure for fragmentation across party groups and countries. Therefore, we intend to explore the effects of the financial crisis in both a national and a supranational context.

Consensus, the Crisis and the Opposition's Choice

The degree of consensus in parliament is the result of two contrasting pressures. One comes from the need of opposition parties to mark their position as distinct from that of other parties. This is a pressure towards conflict, which pushes political parties to signal their distance from the government's policy positions. The other is a force towards cooperation that comes from the need of government to ensure large support for their policies, echoed by the opposition's wish to take part in the decision-making and influence policy decisions. In sum, consensus in parliament is the result of the balance between a tendency towards conflict and another towards cooperation. As a rule, the latter prevails: at national level, an extremely high level of consensus in the lawmaking process has been found in almost all the European parliamentary democracies (Andeweg, De Winter, & Müller, 2008; Christiansen & Damgaard, 2008; Cowley & Stuart, 2005; Giuliani, 2008; Kaiser, 2008; M|újica & Sánchez-Cuenca, 2006). This is true to such an extent that parties generally are 'in opposition, in the sense of being out of government, but not necessarily in disagreement on a continuing basis with government' (Norton, 2008, p. 241). At supranational level, within the EP, a similar pressure to choose between conflict and cooperation across parties is visible. On the one hand, MEPs have incentives to act cohesively to maximise their chances of being influential, or simply to pass legislation as often an absolute majority is required. On the other, party lines, nationalities and government–opposition dynamics are drivers of conflict. As observed in national parliaments, however, cooperation prevails in the EP: on average, about two-thirds of legislation is passed with the consensus of a 'grand coalition' composed of the European Popular Party (EPP), the Party of European Socialists (PES), and the Liberals.[3]

With the financial crisis, the opposition parties' usual dilemma between conflict and cooperation has become particularly intricate. At the national level, the difficulty of borrowing for most European countries – and for some, the conditions of the loan set by the European Central Bank (ECB), the International Monetary Fund (IMF) and the European Commission (EC) – forces governments to make radical changes in their policies, notably in areas such as taxation, pensions, labour policy, and the like. Austerity measures are by their very nature unpopular and, as stated by classical economic voting theory, in bad economic times voters are much more likely to withdraw their support for the government (Healy & Lenz, 2013; Lewis-Beck, 1988). This 'golden rule' has not been disproved by the current crisis: in 2011 we witnessed the fall of the incumbents in all the main countries of southern Europe.[4] As noted by Bosco and Verney, governments are always 'wrong' in these critical situations.

> The economic storm that has broken out in Southern Europe has shown that when incumbents are 'responsible' – abiding by the agreements with the external actors – they end up neglecting their voters' demands ... On the other hand, when incumbents avoid being 'responsible' and/or try to be primarily responsive to their voters, they lose international credibility, with dangerous consequences for the management of national sovereign debt and hence for the economic health of the country. (Bosco & Verney, 2012, p. 133)

These two extremes are well-represented by the cases of Zapatero's government in Spain, on the one hand, and that led by Berlusconi in Italy, on the other. The first fell because his voters felt betrayed, while the second had to resign because he had not acted responsibly enough to ensure the required financial stability for his country. The political opportunities of opposition parties in such a critical scenario are thus conflicting: they have a choice between the need to cooperate with the majority to influence the direction of far-reaching socio-economic changes in order to overcome the crisis, and the chance to weaken a fragile government even further and possibly get into power if elections are held. While the executive has to act responsibly, deepening the tension between its representative and governing function in favour of the latter (Mair, 2011), the opposition parties can often grant themselves the luxury not to.

A similar reasoning can be made at the supranational level. On the one hand, the decisions taken at the EU level following the crisis are urgent, extremely relevant and are the result of difficult negotiations between the member states, so that the MEPs are inclined to act consensually for their country's sake. In addition, many of these decisions have been passed at intergovernmental level, out of the traditional legislative procedure. As the literature shows, in many cases the EP has acted as a competence maximiser (Farrell & Héritier, 2007; H|éritier, Moury, Bischoff, & Bergström, 2013; Moury, 2007), that is, it aims to maximise its influence on the decision-making process. All these factors have encouraged the EP to act cohesively, in order to ensure a quick and safe passage of these measures and/or increase its influence on them. But on the other hand, the crisis has also generated a strong pressure towards conflict. First, socio-economic measures and reforms taken in response to the crisis are very ideological and entail considerable delegation at the EU level. As a consequence, they are likely to split the EP across party lines (left/right and pro/anti-EU integration). Second, the recent socio-economic measures entail very different costs and benefits for the different member states according to whether they are creditors or lenders, or whether they belong to the eurozone or not. This would also promote new divisions within the EP along geographical lines. As a consequence, we expect the dilemma between conflict and cooperation also to be relevant within the EP.

Preliminary Research Hypotheses

Little is said in the existing literature about the possible conduct of parliamentary parties given such an extreme quandary. Traditionally, consensus in parliament has been thought to be affected by the characteristics of the political system in which the opposition parties operate, such as the type of government, type of parties and party competition and institutional resources (Duverger, 1951; Oberreuter, 1975; Pulzer, 1987; Sartori, 1966). Typologies of opposition based on the mentioned systemic factors are still functional and effective, yet they rely on models based on an ideal image of democracy that still exists in theory, but no longer corresponds to the actual performance of political actors (Andeweg et al., 2008; Cowley & Stuart, 2005; Giuliani, 2008; Kaiser, 2008; Mújica & Sánchez-Cuenca, 2006). Consensus in parliament has been proved to be affected also by non-systemic variables such as the preferences of the political actors, the characteristics of the legislation to be approved and, in particular, the policy area involved (De Giorgi, 2011; Green-Pedersen, 2007; Jenkins, 2010; Rose, 1984; Tsebelis, 2002).

What is particularly relevant in our case is that the opposition parties' behaviour in parliament has been proved to be more adversarial on economic and social policies, as parties are expected to represent different socio-economic interests, while the highest level of consensus is usually found on matters of national interest commonly affecting the whole electorate, such as foreign affairs and defence (Rose, 1984). The idea that 'policy determines politics', that the nature of issues entails distinct patterns of cooperation and conflict (Lowi, 1972; Wilson, 1980), points to the relevance of issue-voting, which has an established tradition among scholars of decision-making and roll-call voting (Clausen, 1973; Erikson, 1978; Francis, 1967; Kuklinski, 1978; Miller & Stokes, 1963). Furthermore, the saliency that parties give to different issues has an impact on their voting behaviour in parliament (Carammia & De Giorgi, 2011; Mújica & Sánchez-Cuenca, 2006; Stecker, 2011): low issue salience suggests lack of attention from the public, hence less incentive for political parties to compete. By contrast, the more a party (and its electorate) assigns relevance to an issue, the more costly it will be to behave consensually. Although the legislation presented by the governments to save their country from the worst effects of the financial crisis might be considered as related to national interests, it is also clearly related to socio-economic issues and innately salient. Hence, we expect the level of consensus between the government and opposition parties to decrease as the number of socio-economic and salient policies discussed in parliament increases.

Moreover, as pointed out in the existing literature, the nature of parties constitutes a crucial variable that also explains the behaviour of the opposition in parliament (Duverger, 1951; Flanagan, 2001; Sartori, 1966). In particular, we expect to find a significant difference between the so-called *radical* parties – that is, parties proposing extreme societal changes which are usually permanently in opposition – and the *mainstream* parties, with a more moderate stance, which usually alternate in government. We expect this difference between permanent and alternative opposition to play a crucial role in the choice either to support or to oppose the economic measures proposed by the governments. As a result, we expect to have two kinds of opposition:[5] that of the mainstream parties – that is, parties with government aspirations, which are waiting to be called to replace the government in office in the near future – will behave in a more cooperative way; while that of the parties permanently excluded from power will radicalise their positions in the legislative arena even further.

In a similar vein, scholars have already worked on the impact of Euroscepticism – and conversely of pro-European attitudes – on the government–opposition dynamics and party competition at national level (Hooghe, Marks, & Wilson, 2004; Sitter, 2001, 2002; Szczerbiak & Taggart, 2003) and on the voting behaviour in the EP (Hix, Noury, & Roland, 2007). In normal times 'virtually every policy area is now affected to a greater or lesser extent by the EU ... National elections are still contested on the basis of policy choices, but policy choices are largely decided in Brussels' (Bulmer & Radaelli, 2004, pp. 2–3). In this period of crisis, this dynamic has been stressed even further. Since the outbreak of the crisis, the EU has acquired a key influence in socio-economic policy areas and has started recommending the measures that are to be approved by the national governments. This has happened in Greece, Ireland, Portugal and Spain, where countries and banks were bailed out and the international lenders – the ECB, IMF and the EC – set conditions for the loan; but also in Italy and more recently in Cyprus. Recommendations tend towards an extremely quick reduction of public debt or deficit, but also indicate a whole series of structural reforms. Even in countries that have not been bailed out, the influence of the EC on the budget draft is undoubtedly substantial. Thus, a clear trend has been registered: an increase in the European influence over (or even a Europeanisation of) the usually controversial sectors of social and economic policy. Given this, we expect the traditionally pro-European parties to be more likely to cooperate than before on socio-economic measures, because they follow the EU recommendations/orders. Alternatively, we expect the Eurosceptic parties to have less incentive than before to collaborate when the EU influences legislation.

Thus, although we expect a general decrease in the level of consensus after the onset of the crisis (due to the rising number of salient and socio-economic policy decisions), we expect the *net* impact of the crisis on the opposition parties' behaviour to vary significantly from one party to another. Since the onset of the crisis, the mainstream and pro-European parties, which usually alternate in government, are expected to behave more consensually than they would have done for similar policies in other circumstances. We expect the contrary to be true for the radical parties. Obviously, these two hypotheses are closely related, as parties that are permanently out of government tend to be more Eurosceptic (Sitter, 2001; Taggart, 1998).[6]

While the first hypotheses apply to both national and European legislative arenas, an additional hypothesis relates to the shift in time in the national context. As stated above, austerity measures are by their nature unpopular and so it is the government that has to implement them. In other words, during the financial crisis the major opposition parties have a better chance of replacing the incumbents in the case of new elections. This idea is consistent with the literature that economic and financial crises tend to lead to government instability and termination (Browne, Frendreis, & Gleiber, 1986).[7] The current crisis is no exception. On the contrary, it has been the rule in nearly all the elections in southern Europe since 2011 to punish the incumbent. Of all the national elections held in the last two years in the four countries under analysis, just one has witnessed the victory of the incumbent: the Portuguese presidential election in early 2011.[8] The impact of the economic crisis on the political development of southern Europe was clear and undoubtedly negative for the incumbents, although this did not always mean a clear victory of the main opposition parties. In fact, in several of the last elections, the incumbent parties' loss did not coincide with the official opposition's gain as would normally have been expected. In Greece, the electoral results were so confused that a further election had to be called soon after that of May 2012. In Spain, despite the 15.1 per cent of the total vote lost by the Spanish Socialist Party, the People's Party increased its own support by only 4.7 per cent (Bosco & Verney, 2012). In Italy, the situation was even worse for the centre-left coalition, which was expected to win easily the election held in February 2013: in fact, the results led to the absence of a majority in the Senate, and the centre-left Democratic Party (PD) was forced to make a post-electoral grand coalition with the main centre-right party, the *Popolo delle Libertà* (PDL) of Silvio Berlusconi. It was only in Portugal in the general election held in 2011 that the increase in the vote for the centre-right PSD exceeded the incumbent socialists' loss. However, even given this variegated picture, the opposition's opportunities in the case of elections are certainly higher than in normal times. Therefore, our final research hypothesis relates to variation in time and across cases, within the same period of crisis. We expect that the more the government is in jeopardy, the greater the opposition's incentives to fight rather than to support the executive. In other words, we posit that, once the financial crisis has begun, the opposition behaves in a more conflictual way when the government's incumbency is at risk, for instance, when it lacks a majority of seats in parliament or its popularity declines, and in a less conflictual way when it is not, that is, when elections have just been held or technocratic governments, rather than true political competitors, are in charge.

The (Economic and Political) Crisis in Southern Europe

We shall test our argument in the four southern European countries that experienced the greatest pressure from the crisis: Portugal, Italy, Greece and Spain. Apart from their geographic proximity, these systems actually share controversial features at both the political and economic levels:

> On the political side, they have often been portrayed as systems characterised by weakly institutionalised party systems, whose electorates nevertheless show restricted electoral volatility, along with ideological voting and extended political patronage. On the economic side, their structures appear weaker than their Northern European counterparts, with uneven economic developments typical of dual economies, large state economic involvement and reduced social mobility. (Bellucci, Costa Lobo, & Lewis-Beck, 2012, p. 470)

The sarcastic acronym PIGS – Portugal, Italy, Greece and Spain[9] – was in fact created to identify those national systems characterised by economic and political weaknesses in Europe. In recent years, those common features have actually led to nearly the same political and economic outcomes: all four countries were hit dramatically by the international economic crisis and had to face a period of political instability at the same time.

Besides these general similarities, there are in fact important differences between the four. In the course of 2011, the prime minister (PM) resigned and the government was replaced in all four countries under analysis. However, this outcome was reached in two different ways: through the call for new elections and the victory of the parties that were previously in opposition in Portugal and Spain; and through the replacement of the PM thanks to the formation of a new parliamentary majority supporting the government without going to the polls, in Greece and Italy. But the latter two governments had different destinies: on the one hand, the new Greek executive led by Lucas Papademos lasted only a few months and was followed by two general elections in rapid succession (in May and June 2012), because the results of the first one did not allow the formation of a stable government. On the other hand, the new Italian executive led by the former EU Commissioner Mario Monti almost completed its parliamentary term. Monti resigned in December 2012 and a new general election was held in February 2013, opening a new (critical) political scenario that resulted in the formation of a new government led by Enrico Letta and supported by a grand coalition, for the first time in the history of the so-called second republic.

On the economic side, Greece was the first EU member state to accept the bailout package, which was agreed with the ECB, IMF and EC in April 2010.

The implications of this agreement were both economic and political. The vote to approve the bailout package and the consequent austerity measures put the cohesion of most parliamentary party groups to a serious test. Many MPs who voted against the party whip, belonging to both the government party – the Panhellenic Socialist Movement (PASOK) – and the opposition parties, were expelled. As the economic crisis deepened and the government support kept declining, the opposition parties had less and less incentive to support the government proposals. When the midterm fiscal plan was presented to the parliament in June 2011, it was supported only by the PASOK. After a cabinet reshuffle, the PM's disastrous announcement of a referendum on the measures to be approved, and ultimately his resignation, a new coalition was formed by the PASOK, the main opposition conservative New Democracy (ND), and the radical right Popular Orthodox Rally (LAOS), at the end of 2011. But this solution was not enough to avoid going back to the polls for too long. Since June 2012, Antonis Samaras has been leading a coalition government supported by a composite majority with PASOK, the democratic left-wing DIMAR and the conservative ND (with a limited role in government).

Although the first months of 2013 in Italy seemed reminiscent of the political impasse that Greece had to face between May and June 2012, the situation was different. Bosco and Verney (2012) had actually predicted that 'the electoral epidemic spreading in Southern Europe' would have included 'the growth of abstention, increasing parliamentary fragmentation and the emergence of new political forces, notably those expressing anti-party, extreme right-wing or even racist positions' (p. 150). In the case of Italy, it was mainly the anti-party sentiment that led to the fall of both the centre-right and centre-left coalition at the election held in February 2013 and resulted in the rise of the Five Stars Movement (*Movimento Cinque Stelle*) founded a few years earlier by the famous comedian and blogger Beppe Grillo, whose list got more than 25 per cent of the votes. This caused the absence of a clear majority in the Senate and thus difficulty in the rapid appointment of a new coalition government. As noted above, the solution was to form a government supported by an unprecedented grand coalition, composed of the traditional political adversaries of the second republic – the centre-left PD and the centre-right PDL – and the new *Lista Civica* led by the former PM Mario Monti. From an economic point of view, Italy has never had to ask for a real bailout, although it has been clear from the start that the executive led by Monti following Berlusconi's resignation had to follow an exact plan agreed at European level in order to overcome the economic crisis that was seriously threatening the country.

Although the economic situation in Portugal and Spain was (and still is) worse than that of Italy, they seem to have acquired greater political stability since the elections of 2011. In Portugal, after the parliament's rejection of an austerity package – the fourth in less than one year – the Socialist PM José Sócrates resigned and international lenders were called to the rescue in April 2011. After that, the centre-right Social Democratic Party (PSD) and the right-wing

Democratic and Social Centre Party (CDS) obtained an absolute majority at the general election held in June. Since that time, however, the new government led by Pedro Passos Coelho has had to act according to the rules agreed at the time of the bailout with the ECB, IMF and EC; the three main parties in parliament (the Socialist Party [PS], PSD and CDS) had taken part in the negotiations and, like the other countries rescued by the international lenders, it was the nation that had made the commitment rather than a particular government (Mair, 2011).

In the Spanish case, the Socialist government implemented the biggest redefinition of the welfare state, including public servant wage cuts, freezing pensions and limiting public debt at both state level and regional level. The new Popular Party government, appointed after the resignation of the Socialist PM José Luis Zapatero and the general election that followed, also implemented policies that contradicted its ideological claims by raising income taxes. In both cases, the political costs were very high.

So how have the opposition parties reacted to this dramatic situation in southern Europe? Have they tried to behave 'responsibly' by cooperating with the government in office, or have they stressed their adversarial position and tried to benefit from the difficulties and low popularity of the leading parties? In this comparative work we shall try to verify our research hypotheses about the possible behaviour of the opposition in such a critical economic and political scenario.

The Crisis in the European Parliament

As we know, the EP does not, *strictu sensu*, have one government and one opposition. But by including the EP in this study, we can further our study of the impact of the crisis on parliamentary cohesion and consensus. As a matter of fact, involving the EP represents a terrific opportunity for such an enterprise from an empirical and theoretical perspective. Empirically, the measures taken at the EU level – fiscal compact, six-pack financial regulations, measures such as the European Financial Stability Facility (EFSF) and European Stability Mechanism (ESM) – are absolutely innovative in terms of policy relevance, but also in terms of the process that led to the decision. Analysing the way in which the EP has passed these extraordinary measures and the manner in which it was able to act cohesively to hold the EU Council and Commission accountable, when the measures needed no passage in parliament, is of fundamental importance to understand how EU democracy functions and its resilience when faced with an unprecedented crisis.

Analysing the impact of the crisis on EP cohesion is also important from a theoretical point of view. Many EU scholars (see Hix & Noury, 2009; Hix et al., 2007) have observed that a large majority of the votes in the EP can be read in terms of MEPs' group affiliation, while only a minority of votes can be explained along national lines. The same authors also observed a shift from consensus to greater division across ideological party lines in the last decade.

As a result, the question that arises is whether the crisis has strengthened this process of 'ideologisation' of the EP, as the measures passed are clearly ideologically marked; or whether it represents a new driving force towards a divide across geographical lines. But more than an enlightening exercise for EU scholars, the inclusion of the EP in this study enables us to check whether the hypotheses made above on the basis of the literature on national legislatures could also apply to the EP. As Hix noted, the EU is a political system and hence it makes great sense to apply the literature developed at the national level to the EU. In fact, the decisions to save the EU from the worst effects of the crisis are of considerable importance, and hence MEPs – particularly those from mainstream parties – might be motivated by the same sense of responsibility and commitment as their national counterparts; on the other hand, radical and Eurosceptic parties might feel an incentive to distance themselves even further from the decisions taken by the mainstream parties in government. From that perspective, the last contribution of this study considers the MEPs to be under similar pressures as their counterparts in national legislatures.

The Work to Follow

In the comparative work that follows, we shall examine the preliminary hypotheses posited above through a qualitative and quantitative analysis of the behaviour of the opposition parties in the four European democracies hit most acutely by the crisis – Greece, Italy, Portugal and Spain – and in the EP. Each contribution will propose a combination of empirical data analysis and qualitative process-tracking, in order to test the hypotheses and/or check for alternative explanations as well as to understand the shift from consensus to dissent, or vice versa, in the opposition behaviour.

Before proceeding, we must underline once more that the relevant political differences among the four cases under analysis – above all, the characteristics, duration and stability of the new governments and the ways that led to the formation of the new executives themselves – do not allow the empirical investigation of the government–opposition dynamics in these countries to be identical. While the immediate elections in Portugal and Spain allowed the voters to assign clear responsibility of the economic situation to the incumbents and led to the victory of the main opposition parties, the technocratic parenthesis in Italy and Greece prevented the electorate from giving the same clear judgement and – together with further country-related factors that will be explored in depth in the works to follow – contributed to the (nebulous) electoral results that we mentioned above and, in both cases, the implosion of the party system. As a consequence, while Portugal and Spain will allow us to test our hypotheses and compare the results, Greece and Italy will be treated slightly differently, as will the EP, given its different supranational nature.

Notes

1. See, among others, Matsaganis (2011, 2012), Navarro (2012) and Royo (2012).
2. See, in particular, the whole Electoral Studies Special Symposium 'Economic Crisis and Elections: The European Periphery', edited by Bellucci et al. (2012), and the *South European Society and Politics* special issue 'Elections in hard times: Southern Europe, 2010–11', edited by Bosco and Verney (2012).
3. Source: VoteWatch.eu for the seventh legislature.
4. It is only in Spain that elections would normally have been called just four months later; the Portuguese, Greek and Italian governments were all close to their midterm point (the parliamentary term is five years in Italy, but four years in Portugal, Greece and Spain).
5. As pointed out by Mair (2011), it seems that 'governing capacity and vocation' have become characteristic of a fairly restricted group of parties that belong to the mainstream of the party system and are able to offer voters a choice of government. On the other hand, the capacity of 'representation', or expression of the people's voice, when it has not moved completely outside the legislative arena, has become the characteristic of a different group of parties. These parties constitute the 'new opposition'. They rarely govern, they are usually distinguished by a strong populist rhetoric and, even if not equal to the anti-system parties of Sartori (1976), they share with those parties a kind of 'semi-responsible', if not completely 'irresponsible', opposition. 'In other words, it is possible to speak of a growing divide in European party systems between parties which claim to represent, but do not deliver, and those which deliver, but are no longer seen to represent' (p. 14). In our opinion, this divide is crucial to the understanding of the government–opposition dynamics during the financial crisis, not just in southern European countries but in all European democracies.
6. It is actually so hard to combine Eurosceptic stances with government ambitions that Eurosceptic parties that want to become credible coalition partners frequently moderate their hostility to Europe (Conti & De Giorgi, 2011; Costa Lobo & Magalhães, 2011).
7. This argument is clearly supported in Portugal, which had already experienced two financial crises that pushed the country into requesting international financial assistance from the IMF in 1978–79 and in 1983–85. Those interventions, like the current one, triggered political instability and early elections.
8. It has to be noted that, although the Constitution gives the Portuguese president quite a strong set of powers, in practice the Portuguese presidents have tended not to use them. As they do not play a direct role in the government of the country, they are therefore less likely to be held responsible for its bad status by the voters.
9. At first, the initial 'I' referred to Italy, then it was linked to Ireland, and since that time sometimes a second 'I' has been added: PI(I)GS.

References

Andeweg, R. B., De Winter, L., & Müller, W. C. (2008). Parliamentary opposition in post-consociational democracies: Austria, Belgium and the Netherlands. *The Journal of Legislative Studies*, *14*(1), 77–112.

Bellucci, P., Costa Lobo, M., & Lewis-Beck, M. S. (2012). Economic crisis and elections: The European periphery. *Electoral Studies*, *31*, 469–471.

Bosco, A., & Verney, S. (2012). Electoral epidemic: The political cost of economic crisis in southern Europe, 2010–11. *South European Society and Politics*, *17*(2), 129–154.

Browne, E. C., Frendreis, J. P., & Gleiber, D. W. (1986). The process of cabinet dissolution: An exponential model of duration and stability in western democracies. *American Journal of Political
Science, 30*, 628–650.

Bulmer, S. J., & Radaelli, C. M. (2004). *The Europeanisation of national policy?* Queen's Papers on
Europeanisation No. 1/2004.

Carammia, M., & De Giorgi, E. (2011, September). *Just empty words? Issue competition in Italy
between rhetoric and legislative behaviour*. Paper presented at the Italian Political Science Association Annual Meeting, Palermo, Italy.

Christiansen, F. J., & Damgaard, E. (2008). Parliamentary opposition under minority parliamentarism:
Scandinavia. *The Journal of Legislative Studies, 14*(1), 46–76.

Clausen, A. (1973). *How Congressmen decide: A policy focus*. New York, NY: St. Martin's Press.

Conti, N., & De Giorgi, E. (2011). Euroscetticismo solo a parole? Lega Nord e Rifondazione comunista,
tra retorica e comportamento istituzionale. *Rivista Italiana di Scienza Politica, 41*(2), 265–290.

Costa Lobo, M., & Magalhães, P. (2011). Room for manoeuvre: Euroscepticism in the Portuguese
parties and electorate (1976–2005). *South European Society and Politics, 16*(1), 81–104.

Cowley, P., & Stuart, M. (2005). Conservatives in unity shocker. Retrieved from http://www.revolts.
co.uk/Conservative%20rebels,%202001-2005.pdf

De Giorgi, E. (2011). L'opposition parlementaire en Italie et au Royaume Uni: Systémique ou axée sur
les enjeux? *Revue Internationale de Politique Comparée, 18*(2), 93–113.

Duverger, M. (1951). *Les parties politiques*. Paris: Colin.

Erikson, R. S. (1978). Constituency opinion and Congressional behavior: A reexamination of the
Miller–Stokes data. *American Journal of Political Science, 22*(3), 511–535.

Farrell, H., & Héritier, A. (2007). Conclusion: Evaluating the forces of interstitial institutional change.
West European Politics, 30(2), 405–415.

Flanagan, T. (2001). *The uneasy case for uniting the right*. Vancouver: Fraser Institute.

Francis, W. L. (1967). *Legislative issues in the fifty states*. Chicago, IL: Rand McNally.

Giuliani, M. (2008). Patterns of consensual law-making in the Italian parliament. *South European
Society and Politics, 13*(1), 61–85.

Green-Pedersen, C. (2007). The growing importance of issue competition: The changing nature of
party competition in western Europe. *Political Studies, 55*(3), 607–628.

Healy, A., & Lenz, J. S. (2013). Substituting the end for the whole: Why voters respond primarily to
the election-year economy. *American Journal of Political Science, 57*(3), 1–17.

Héritier, A., Moury, C., Bischoff, C., & Bergström, C. F. (2013). *Changing rules of delegation. A
contest for power in comitology*. Oxford: Oxford University Press.

Hix, S., & Noury, A. (2009). After enlargement: Voting patterns in the sixth European Parliament.
Legislative Studies Quarterly, 34(2), 159–174.

Hix, S., Noury, A., & Roland, G. (2006). Dimensions of politics in the European Parliament. *American
Journal of Political Science, 50*(2), 494–511.

Hix, S., Noury, A., & Roland, G. (2007). *Democratic politics in the European Parliament*. Cambridge,
MA: Cambridge University Press.

Hooghe, L., Marks, G., & Wilson, C. (2004). Does left/right structure party positions on European
integration? In G. Marks & M. Steenbergen (Eds.), *European integration and political conflict*
(pp. 120–140). Cambridge, MA: Cambridge University Press.

Jenkins, S. (2010). Examining the influence over roll call voting in multiple issue areas: A comparative US state analysis. *Journal of Legislative Studies, 16*(1), 14–31.

Kaiser, A. (2008). Parliamentary opposition in Westminster democracies: Britain, Canada, Australia
and New Zealand. *The Journal of Legislative Studies, 14*(1), 20–45.

Kuklinski, J. H. (1978). Representativeness and elections: A policy analysis. *American Political
Science Review, 72*(1), 165–177.

Lewis-Beck, M. S. (1988). *Economics and elections: The major western democracies*. Ann Arbor, MI:
University of Michigan Press.

Lowi, T. J. (1972). Four systems of policy, politics, and choice. *Public Administration Review, 32*(4),
298–310.

Mair, P. (2011). *Bini Smaghi vs. the parties: Representative government and institutional constraints*
(EUI Working Paper No. 2011/22). Florence: Robert Schuman Centre for Advanced Studies and
EU Democracy Observatory, European University Institute.

Matsaganis, M. (2011). The welfare state and the crisis: The case of Greece. *Journal of European
Social Policy, 21*(5), 501–513.

Matsaganis, M. (2012). Social policy in hard times: The case of Greece. *Critical Social Policy, 32*(3), 406–421.

Miller, W. E., & Stokes, D. E. (1963). Constituency influence in Congress. *American Political Science Review, 57*(1), 45–56.

Moury, C. (2007). Explaining the European Parliament's right to appoint and invest the commission. *West European Politics, 30*(2), 367–391.

Mújica, A., & Sánchez-Cuenca, I. (2006). Consensus and parliamentary opposition: The case of Spain. *Government and Opposition, 41*(1), 86–108.

Navarro, V. (2012). The crisis and fiscal policies in the peripheral countries of the eurozone. *International Journal of Health Services, 42*(1), 1–7.

Norton, P. (2008). Making sense of opposition. *The Journal of Legislative Studies, 14*(1), 236–250.

Oberreuter, H. (Ed.). (1975). *Parlamentarische Opposition. Ein Internationaler Vergleich*. Hamburg: Hoffman and Campe.

Pulzer, P. (1987). Is there life after Dahl? In E. Kolinsky (Ed.), *Opposition in western Europe* (pp. 10–30). London and Sidney: Croom Helm.

Rose, R. (1984). *Do parties make a difference?* London: Macmillan Press.

Royo, S. (2012). How did the Spanish financial system survive the first stage of the global crisis? *Governance, 26*(4), 631–656.

Sartori, G. (1966). Opposition and control: Problems and prospects. *Government and Opposition, 1*(2), 149–154.

Sartori, G. (1976). *Parties and party systems. A framework for analysis*. Cambridge, MA: Cambridge University Press.

Sitter, N. (2001). The politics of opposition and European integration in Scandinavia: Is Euro-scepticism a government–opposition dynamic? *West European Politics, 24*(4), 22–39.

Sitter, N. (2002), *Opposing Europe: Euro-scepticism, opposition and party competition* (SEI Working Paper No. 56 and OERN Working Paper No. 9). Brighton: Sussex European Institute, University of Sussex.

Stecker, C. (2011, September). *Voting patterns of the parliamentary opposition in Germany*. Paper presented at the Italian Political Science Association Annual Meeting, Palermo, Italy.

Szczerbiak, A., & Taggart P. (2003, March). *Theorising party-based Euroscepticism: Problems of definition*. Paper presented at the European Union Studies Association International Conference, Nashville, TN.

Taggart, P. (1998). A touchstone of dissent: Euroscepticism in contemporary western European party systems. *European Journal of Political Research, 33*(3), 363–388.

Tsebelis, G. (2002). *Veto players: How political institutions work*. Princeton, NJ: Princeton University Press.

Wilson, J. Q. (Ed.). (1980). *The politics of regulation*. New York, NY: Basic Books.

Government–Opposition Dynamics during the Economic Crisis in Greece

KOSTAS GEMENIS and ROULA NEZI

This contribution examines the turbulent period of 2010–12 when Greece became the first European Union member state to accept the International Monetary Fund/European Union bailout package, which had significant electoral consequences. The May 2012 election was characterised by unprecedented electoral volatility and a reshuffling of the party system. An understanding of this development is sought by focusing on the relationship between government and opposition parties in terms of their MPs' legislative voting behaviour on key economic bills in the aforementioned period. It is observed that although the economic crisis seems to have decreased the importance of the traditional left–right dimension, the bailout agreements reinforced the conflict between the responsive and responsible aspects of representative government and created a new conflict dimension over supporters and opponents of the bailout agreements. This contribution concludes with a call to reassess the impact of European integration on national party systems.

Introduction

When George Papandreou, leader of the Panhellenic Socialist Movement (PASOK), was elected as prime minister of Greece in October 2009, few would have expected what would follow. Even though the consequences of the global financial crisis were already looming large for Greece after the June 2009 election to the European Parliament (EP), Papandreou's promise of a three billion euro stimulus package for the economy implied that the country could continue into the crisis doing business as usual (Gemenis, 2010, p. 360). These prospects were quickly abandoned, however, when the PASOK government realised that the country's debt was spiralling out of control and negotiated a bailout package with the representatives of the European Commission (EC), the European Central Bank (ECB), and the International Monetary Fund (IMF), collectively known as the *troika*. In this conjuncture, the opposition parties were faced with a dilemma. They could either support the government's decision and attempt to build a wider consensus around implementing the reforms mandated by the lenders, or oppose the government, hoping that they would be able to benefit electorally from the ensuing dissatisfaction. Whether parties would choose one way or another was not only based on strategic considerations but also necessitated by ideological constraints.

This contribution begins with a brief description of the post-1981 party system and the nature of party competition in Greece. The description is based on a presentation of expert survey data on party positions that show how party competition in Greece has been steadily evolving from a one-dimensional representation to a more complex structure involving several cross-cutting dimensions of contestation. Up to the time of the economic crisis, however, these were not considered to be particularly salient compared with the classic debate on state involvement in the economy. The contribution continues with an analysis based on an extensive narrative that describes voting patterns in the Greek parliament during the period 2010–12. The narrative focuses on the most important conjectures of the bailout agreements and shows how the strategic considerations of party leaders relating to the dilemma between responsive and responsible aspects of representative government (Mair, 2013) were at odds with the emerging conflict over the bailout agreements. The narrative shows how this incongruity created fissures within the established political parties and led to the formation of splinter parties over the bailout agreements conflict. As the pre-2010 aspects of party competition and the friction over the bailout agreements cannot fully explain the implosion of the party system that took place a few months prior to the May 2012 election, this contribution points to a complementary explanation. It argues that the bailout agreements strengthened the importance of certain aspects, such as European integration (Hooghe, Marks, & Wilson, 2002), that distinguish the centripetal political forces from the extreme right and left parties. Although the argument is based on the analysis of a single country, this contribution highlights some previously unexplored mechanisms regarding the impact of Europe in domestic politics.

Party Competition and the Party System since 1981

Since 1981, and up to the period examined here, the Greek party system has been characterised by the dominance of two parties that have alternated in power as well as a smaller pool consisting of parties of the left (Nicolacopoulos, 2005; Pappas, 2003). Like many other parliamentary democracies in western Europe, the two major parties were initially created on the premise of competing on the opposing sides of an economy defined by income redistribution and the degree of state intervention in the economy. PASOK was founded in 1974 and, in many respects, exemplified the programmatic trajectories of social democratic parties in Europe, while New Democracy (ND), founded the same year, followed a similar route to many conservative (and sometimes) Christian democratic parties. The Communist Party of Greece (KKE) dominated the political spectrum to the left of PASOK by adopting more radical, but less electorally popular, stances on this economic dimension. Moreover, more often than not issues regarding morality, post-materialist, or the nationalist versus cosmopolitan conflict, were subsumed into the aforementioned left–right clash. Parties on the left tended to adopt more permissive and cosmopolitan positions than parties on the right. Whatever exceptions to this rule existed, they were too small to alter the pattern of one-dimensional competition radically, as commentators of Greek politics have often pointed out (Lyrintzis, 2005).

The centripetal strategies of the two main parties, especially after the post-1992 era, which undeniably limited the governing parties' space for manoeuvring their economic policies, led to a blurring of ideological boundaries between the two main parties and created opportunities for the formation of new parties. PASOK and ND responded to this challenge by setting up what exemplified, in many respects, a 'cartel' (Katz & Mair, 1995) party system, where the constituent parties of the cartel have been increasingly relying on state funding, media regulation, and manipulation of the electoral system to secure access to office. For instance, parties in office have not only controlled the state media, but also regulated the private market in a way that makes it dependent upon political patronage (Papatheodorou & Machin, 2003). Greece is also one of the first among consolidated democracies to tailor changes to the electoral system to suit their needs, as PASOK and ND have often done.[1]

Figure 1 presents the evolution of party competition in Greece along two conflict axes: the economic axis over state involvement in the economy (higher values indicate support for the free market) and the social 'libertarian versus authoritarian' axis (where higher values indicate an authoritarian placement). The data on party positions come from the 1999, 2002, 2006 and 2010 Chapel Hill Expert Surveys (Bakker et al., 2012), whereas the size of the circles in the plots represents the electoral strength of the parties (in the 1996, 2000, 2004 and 2009 national elections, respectively).[2] As can be seen in Figure 1, until 1999, party positions could be neatly projected on to a one-dimensional 'socio-economic' left–right dimension. By 2002, the cartelisation strategy of the two main parties had resulted in the electoral demise of Political Spring (POLAN, a ND splinter) and the Democratic Social Movement (DIKKI, a PASOK splinter). In the following years, the move of the KKE towards a more socially conservative position, the transformation of the 'Euro-Communist' Coalition of the Left and Progress (SYN) into the radical left Coalition of the Radical Left (SYRIZA) and the emergence of the radical right Popular Orthodox Rally (LAOS) challenged the dimensionality of party competition in Greece (Gemenis & Dinas, 2010). By 2010, the weakening of the two main parties (Dinas, 2010) and the emergence of the Ecologist Greens (ECO) (Gemenis, 2009) meant that the space of political competition had virtually turned two-dimensional, which can be seen by the change in the slope of the weighted regression line in the plots.

A similar pattern emerges when it comes to European integration (see Figure 2). Although party positions have been shown to be orthogonal to the socio-economic left–right dimension at the European level, with moderate parties being in favour of European integration and extreme left and right parties being against (Hooghe et al., 2002), the picture in Greece was rather different. Up to 1999, party positions on European integration were neatly aligned with those on the

Figure 1: Party Positions on the Economic and Social Dimensions of Party Competition

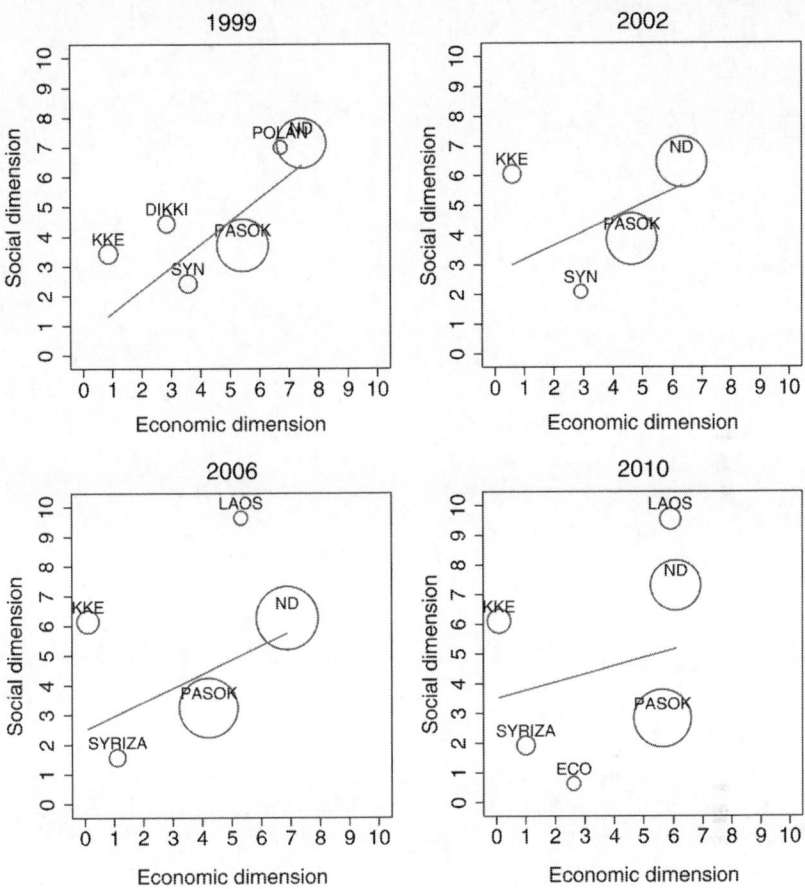

Notes: Size of circles indicates electoral strength; fit line weighted by electoral strength.

(socio-economic) left–right dimension. By 2002, KKE remained the only true Eurosceptic party, something that reflected the rise in public support for European integration (Verney, 2011). By 2006, however, the creation of SYRIZA by SYN and the emergence of LAOS added Eurosceptic parties to both sides of the left–right spectrum (Vasilopoulou, 2011). As the permissive consensus over European integration was gradually replaced by a constraining dissensus (Hooghe & Marks, 2008), ND seems to have adopted a slightly more critical stance as well. With the addition of the rather pro-EU Greens into the competition, party positions in Greece reached the familiar 'inverted-U' relationship between European integration and left–right competition.

So far the evidence from the expert surveys on party positions, as well as evidence from party manifestos (see Teperoglou & Tsatsanis, 2011), shows that,

Figure 2: Party Positions on the Left–Right and European Integration Dimensions

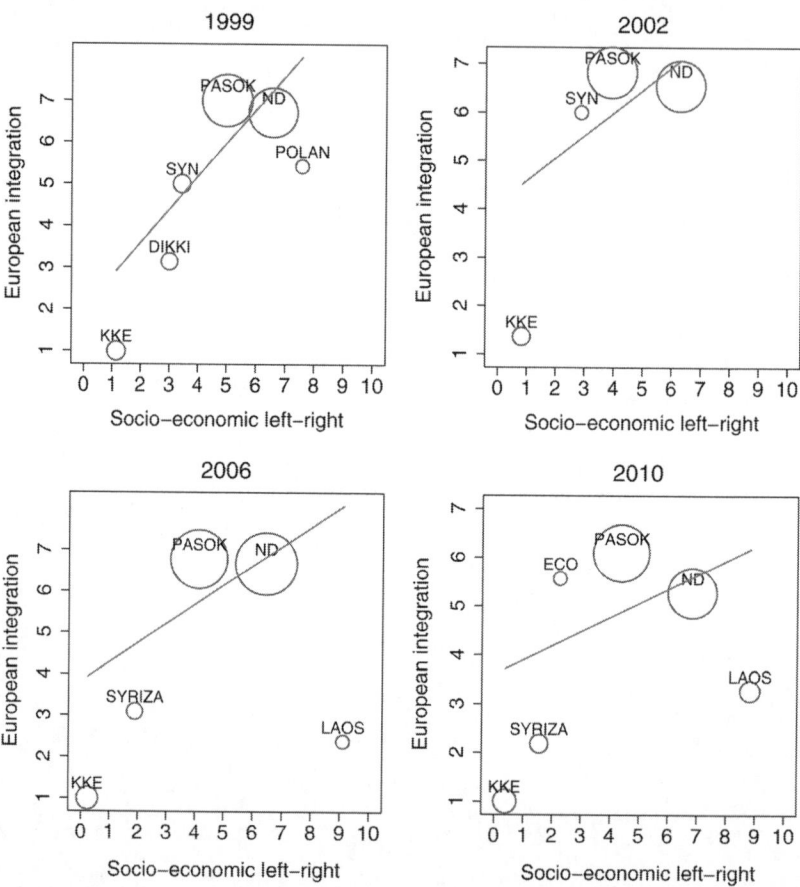

Notes: Size of circles indicates electoral strength; fit line weighted by electoral strength.

despite the cartelisation of the party system, party competition in Greece has gradually been evolving to encompass more than one aspect. It is nevertheless important to note that the emerging aspects are not comparable to the economic one in terms of their salience. The economy has always been perceived as being more important by the electorate compared with social issues or European integration (see Nezi, 2012). In the following section, however, we show how the economic crisis has opened up the potential for increasing the salience of contestation over European integration, and argue that Greece's acceptance of the EU/IMF bailout agreement has created a new conflict in the Greek parliament between supporters and opponents of the agreement. Our narrative outlines how the conflict cross-cuts the traditional government versus opposition pattern of legislative voting in the Greek parliament and how the handling of this new conflict by the party whips created fissures within established parties and opportunities for the creation of splinter parties.

Legislative Voting during the Economic Crisis

Until 2010, voting patterns in the Greek parliament could be understood in terms of the cartelised party system consisting of parties with weak ideological cohesion but strong discipline. The weak ideological cohesion was due to the strategy of the two parties to capture power by attracting candidates not on the basis of their ideological compactness, but on the size of their political clientele (Pappas, 2009). Contrary to the western European experience, PASOK did not only rely upon its ideology to win elections during the 1980s. As the party did not have a long or consolidated relationship with the trade unions that traditionally formed the backbone of social democratic parties in Western Europe, it increasingly relied on polarising discourse, populism and patronage to establish itself electorally as well as targeting floating voters (Kalyvas, 1997; Mavrogordatos, 1997; Pappas, 2010). Partially in response to PASOK's strategies and partially in response to demands within its own constituencies, the strategy of ND with regard to patronage has been largely similar (Close, 2009; Pappas & Assimakopoulou, 2012). In addition, the strategy of ND to absorb many cadres of the extreme right after the 1977 election contributed not only to the virtual extinction of the extreme right until the late 1990s, but also to the formation of a visible faction within ND that was often at odds with the centrist party leadership (Pappas & Dinas, 2006).

Despite the ideological heterogeneity, the lack of electoral prospects outside the major parties meant that 'loyalty' was often less costly than 'voice', let alone 'exit'. It became apparent that, if PASOK and ND MPs disagreed with their parties, the only successful exit solution was to cross the floor to the other major party of the cartel. As a result, as Sotiropoulos (2012) notes, the Greek parliament was characterised by 'the tradition of strong discipline, resulting in the expulsion of dissidents by the party leadership . . . while bills of law are rarely if ever rejected by the parliament' (p. 42). Under these terms, one would expect to see legislative voting patterns that are characteristic of majoritarian democracies where the bills supported by a government majority are pitted against a united opposition. The voting patterns during the period 2010–12, however, became more complex (for a chronology of the most important events during this period, see Table A2 in the Appendix).

The Vote on the Memorandum of Understanding, May 2010

Approximately one month after the 2009 election, officials in the PASOK government realised that the budget deficit was about 9 per cent higher than originally expected. This meant that PASOK had to abandon its ambitious plans for a stimulus package, but also that it had to come up with a short-term solution because the country's bonds were quickly downgraded to 'junk' status.

19

Papandreou, having quickly dismissed the option of an outright default, rallied for the creation of a support mechanism within the EU which would offer a bailout package in order to secure the necessary liquidity on the promise of swift reforms (Gemenis, 2010, pp. 360–361). Even if the Greek government was, at the time, making promises that it could not swiftly deliver, Europe miscalculated the problem and gave a slow response (Tsarouhas, 2012, pp. 92–93). The IMF and EU partners were mistaken in thinking that Greece's debt could be managed solely by implementing reforms and without radical restructuring. As a consequence, the memorandum of understanding with the *troika* that was brought to the parliament was seen as a desperate act. For policy-seeking parties there was no chance of debating, let alone changing, the substance of the submitted bill. In this 'take it or leave it' situation, those who thought that Papandreou had done a bad job in the negotiations were more than likely to vote against the bill. Those who did not necessarily consider liberal reforms as undesirable were left to wonder how the policy proposals could be implemented in a *société bloquée*, a society that vehemently opposed reforms (Featherstone, 2005). Nevertheless, in line with the responsible conceptualisation of government, they acknowledged that, even if the measures were poorly formulated and unlikely to be implemented, voting in favour of the bill would be necessary to ensure short-term financial liquidity and the continued presence of the country in the eurozone.

Voting for the memorandum therefore exhibited a peculiar set of accords (see Table 1). Out of the 159 PASOK MPs present, 156 voted according to the party line, and three abstained. The three who abstained were quickly expelled from the parliamentary caucus and the party for not following the party whip; all three, known to have been to the left wing of the party, seeing quite critically the ideological trajectory of the party after Costas Simitis had taken over the party leadership in 1996.

If the behaviour of these three MPs was ideologically motivated, claiming thus to be responsive to their constituents, one cannot conclude entirely the same for the voting instructions issued by ND. Ideologically, ND was far from the social democratic traditions of opposing (neo-)liberal reforms. Nevertheless, the new leader, Antonis Samaras, who emerged after the 2009 defeat, was known for his nationalist stance on foreign policy issues. Signing the memorandum was seen as a national humiliation and, as Samaras had the reputation of someone who felt strongly about 'national' issues, it made sense to oppose the bill. This explanation, however, disregards the fact that, although many ND MPs exhibited a similar attitude with regard to issues of national identity (Nezi, Sotiropoulos, & Toka, 2010), such views were not shared among those with a liberal background, such as Dora Bakoyannis, who voted in favour and was subsequently expelled from the party. Sensing that Bakoyannis's open disagreement with the party line had more to do with an ongoing personal feud (as she was Samaras's main opponent in his November 2009 bid for the ND leadership), rather than create a deep rift in the party, he may have found it preferable to use the party whip as an opportunity to consolidate his leadership. Sacrificing a dissenting

Table 1: Legislative Voting in Key Bills and Events

	1st Memorandum (May 2010)				Midterm Fiscal Plan (June 2011)				Papademos Cabinet (November 2011)				2nd Memorandum (February 2012)			
	Yes	No	Abs.	n/p	Yes	No	Abs.	n/p	Yes	No	Abs.	n/p	Yes	No	Abs.	n/p
PASOK	156		3	1	154	1			148	2		2	129	12	4	7
ND	1	89		1		83		2	83	1		1	63	20		1
SYRIZA		12		1		9				9				9		
KKE		20		1		21				18		3		21		
LAOS	15					15			16				2			14
Dem. Left						4			4	3		1	3	4		
Dem. Alliance							5								1	
ANEL								2	2	5				2		
Ind. Ex-PASOK					1	3			2				2	6		
Ind. Ex-ND																
Total:	172	121	3	4	155	136	5	4	255	38		7	199	74	5	22

Abs. = Abstentions, n/p = not present.

MP should not have serious repercussions if other liberal-minded MPs were unlikely to join her.

To this, we should add an important strategic consideration. In October 2009, ND suffered its worst defeat in parliamentary elections since 1974, while for the first couple of months of 2010 the opinion polls were still giving a considerable lead to PASOK (Gemenis, 2012, p. 109). Considering that in times of economic downturns retrospective evaluations of the economy are expected to hurt the incumbent parties more than the challengers (Nezi, 2012), Samaras might have considered that staying firmly in the opposition would be a sensible thing to do. Knowing that his party would eventually come to deal with similar policy dilemmas as an incumbent, Samaras tried to balance responsiveness and responsibility by presenting his opposition to the bill, arguing that the memorandum was unnecessarily humiliating and presenting an alternative policy plan for overcoming the debt crisis (entitled 'Zappeio').

One would expect that LAOS's voting instructions would have mimicked the ones given in ND. If anything, LAOS was considerably more Eurosceptic than ND (Verney, 2011) and had a tendency to advance conspiracy theories regarding 'foreign interests' and 'enemies of Greece' (Gemenis & Dinas, 2010, p. 190). Opposing the bill would easily fit into the party's ideological trajectory, so the explanation of the affirmative vote should examine the party's goals. Even though LAOS can be primarily characterised as a vote-seeking party (considering the 3 per cent that was necessary for its survival), the party often exhibited office-seeking tendencies. Its leader, Georgios Karatzaferis, had twice previously offered his support to ND, once before the 2007 election (Gemenis, 2008, p. 97), and once in the summer of 2009 when the opinion polls indicated that support for ND was evaporating. Both proposals were rebuffed by the former ND leader Karamanlis, who followed a centripetal ideological trajectory, so Karatzaferis reinstated his office aspirations by playing on the responsible party concept. Finally, as expected, both KKE and SYRIZA voted against the memorandum because they were staunch opponents of both the idea of a bailout plan as well as the reforms proposed therein.

The Vote on the Midterm Fiscal Plan, June 2011

The vote on the memorandum was followed by an important development within SYN, the largest constituent party of the SYRIZA coalition. During the party's June 2010 congress, most of the prominent members of the pro-European integration *Ananeotiki* faction walked out and announced their intention to form a new political party. The dissenters opposed SYN's proposal to transform the SYRIZA electoral coalition into a party as they felt that they would be further marginalised within the new party structure, a disagreement that can be traced back to the struggle over the list for the 2009 EP election (Gemenis, 2010, p. 355). *Ananeotiki* felt that, by merging into a coalition consisting primarily of actors who opposed European integration, SYN was compromising the party's long-standing Europeanism. The new splinter party, named the

Democratic Left, was founded on 27 June 2010 and included four MPs who defected from the SYRIZA parliamentary caucus.

The next test for the government was the regional elections, which were scheduled for November 2010. The contest featured elections for mayors as well as the newly instituted direct election of the 13 regional governors, an office with high visibility but minimal impact on policymaking (Gemenis, 2012, pp. 107–108). Although local and regional elections are traditionally seen as second-order elections in Greece, PASOK feared that the opposition could effectively focus the campaign on the issue of the memorandum. As the Greek Constitution prohibits parties from participating in local and regional elections, the latter take place by creating seemingly independent lists that are nevertheless openly endorsed by parties (Gemenis, 2012, pp. 107–108). One of PASOK's dissenting MPs, who had been expelled in May, Alexis Dimaras, announced that he would contest the most populous Attica region, which includes Athens metropolitan area, while ND had to face some rebels of its own in Crete where a governor candidate was tacitly supported by Bakoyannis. LAOS followed a strategy of fielding experienced candidates of its own in some regions while supporting ND candidates in others, playing on the image of a responsible party which avoided the extreme anti-memorandum overtones, but it found it difficult to support its decision to vote in favour of the memorandum in the course of the campaign and suffered considerable losses (Gemenis, 2012, p. 112). The left opposition of KKE and SYRIZA fared considerably better save for a SYRIZA rebel list in Attica headed by its former leader who had long expressed his dissatisfaction with the present leader, Alexis Tsipras (Gemenis, 2010, p. 356).

In the immediate aftermath of the 2010 elections Bakoyannis announced that she would create a new party. The party, which was founded on 21 November and named Democratic Alliance (DISY), served not only as a vehicle for Bakoyannis's personal ambitions, but also as the latest attempt to create a liberal party headed by an established politician. Within the next two months, four more MPs and one member of the EP crossed the floor and joined the Democratic Alliance, thus reducing the ND parliamentary caucus to 86 members. Within a year, the memorandum vote had not only challenged the popularity of the government and the unity of PASOK, but also created visible fissures among the parties that opposed it. With the exception of KKE, both ND and SYRIZA experienced the creation of moderate splinters that challenged their strategies facing the memorandum.

As it seemed that the government might be able to proceed with another round of austerity measures, a wave of peaceful protests swept the country. Even though strikes and protests had become a regular occurrence in Athens since early 2010, the size of the protests beginning in May 2011 was unprecedented (Sotiropoulos, 2012, pp. 32–33). Prompted by rumours (that later proved to be unsubstantiated) that the *indignados* in Madrid had been ridiculing the Greeks for being passive to the austerity measures, the Greek *indignados*, or '*aganaktismenoi*', gathered at

Syntagma square in Athens. The sit-ins quickly spread to other major cities across Greece and lasted for more than two months.

When the government put the midterm fiscal plan to the vote in the parliament in June, it had become clear that support for the government had evaporated. A cabinet reshuffle on 17 June did not contribute to changing the climate. Those who saw their quality of life deteriorating from the repeated cuts in salaries and pensions, tax hikes, spiralling unemployment (especially among young people), and increase in crime, turned into an angry crowd that threatened to storm the parliament building. Georgios Lianis, a PASOK MP, resigned the party whip after making known that he did not agree with the proposed plan. Counting another MP who resigned the whip a few months earlier, the PASOK parliamentary caucus was reduced to 155 members. Samaras also instructed his 85 MPs to vote against the bill. They all complied apart from Elsa Papadimitriou, who announced her intention to leave the ND caucus and vote in favour, citing the need to avoid the country's quick default. Sensing that public opinion had turned violently against those who supported the memorandum, Bakoyannis and her four Democratic Alliance MPs decided to abstain, whereas Karatzaferis made a U-turn and joined the parties of the left which all voted against, sensing that supporting the bill amidst the massive protests would be electoral suicide for his small party. With an additional PASOK MP voting against the party line, the midterm fiscal plan was voted on a narrow majority (see Table 1).

The Vote on the Papademos Coalition Government, November 2011

After the vote on the midterm fiscal plan it became apparent that the opposition would be unwilling to support any bill brought by the government. PASOK suffered tremendously in the opinion polls and so did the parties that had supported or tolerated the bills in one way or another. The lack of pro-government consensus, however, worried European leaders, and particularly the conservatives in the European People's Party who expected Samaras to support the austerity measures that were tied to the loans to Greece, for which they had been painfully rallying in the parliaments of their own countries ('Antonis Samaras stunned Europe,' 2011; Van Versendaal, 2011).

Playing on the responsible leader image, and resuming his office-seeking strategy, Karatzaferis tried to broker an agreement between Papandreou and Samaras to form an extraordinary coalition government of 'national unity' that would address the country's most pressing problems. His effort, however, was merely an unsuccessful bid for office that was not taken seriously. When another package of austerity measures was brought to the parliament on 20 October, the voting patterns were similar to those of the midterm fiscal plan a few months earlier, save Louka Katseli, a PASOK MP and former minister, who voted against the party line and was subsequently expelled from the parliamentary caucus.

Papandreou then came up with a highly controversial proposal: to bring Greece's bailout plan to a referendum. Apparently, the idea was to rally as much opposition support as possible by thinking that few would like to be responsible for the country's default in the event of a rejection of the bailout. Foreign leaders in the eurozone, however, castigated Papandreou for his bold proposal by arguing that the referendum would jeopardise all their efforts thus far. Moreover, law experts could not decide whether Greece could put the ongoing bailout to a referendum or whether the referendum should instead be about Greece exiting the eurozone. Most importantly, the proposal for a referendum triggered fissures within PASOK, with a further MP declaring her resignation from the parliamentary caucus, reducing PASOK's representation to a hair-splitting majority of 152 MPs. Papandreou then abandoned the idea of a referendum and called for a parliamentary vote of confidence, which received 153 votes (including one from Katseli, who returned to the PASOK caucus).

Sensing that his government had reached its limit only two years after it was brought to power, Papandreou announced to President Karolos Papoulias his intention to form an oversized coalition government. President Papoulias coordinated the coalition talks by inviting the opposition parties. Samaras, who had since considered the pressure from his fellow leaders in the European Popular Party (EPP) to abandon the politics of unqualified opposition, agreed to support a government under the leadership of Lucas Papademos, a former vice-president of the ECB. Apart from the cabinet portfolios received by ND, Samaras's major pay-off was the promise that the duration of the coalition government would not exceed six months and that an election would be held immediately afterwards. Moreover, in order to minimise the electoral cost associated with incumbency during times of crisis (Nezi, 2012), he asked those ND MPs holding cabinet portfolios to resign their seats. Samaras then argued that, technically, ND could not be considered as a partner of the coalition government, hoping that his party would emerge as the winner in the subsequent election. Karatzaferis also supported the coalition but insisted that the government should include a limited number of extra-parliamentary technocrats. In addition, Bakoyannis announced that the Democratic Alliance would support the Papademos government without formal or informal participation in the cabinet.

The resulting cabinet was particularly large compared with its predecessors, with ND contributing two ministers, one deputy minister and three junior ministers, and LAOS one minister, one deputy minister and two junior ministers. Unlike the Monti cabinet in Italy, the Papademos cabinet could only loosely be labelled technocrat. The ratio of six (including Papademos) out of 48 members was just slightly higher than the four out of 36 in the first Papandreou cabinet, implying that portfolios were allocated primarily on the basis of intra-party bargaining for office. On 15 November the Papademos government passed an investiture vote (see Table 1) with 255 MPs in favour, including the combined votes of PASOK, ND, LAOS and Democratic Alliance, as well as many dissenters from PASOK and ND who had resigned the whip or had otherwise been expelled from the parliamentary caucuses.

Once again, two MPs from PASOK, and Panos Kammenos from ND, voted against the party line and were expelled by the party leaders.

The Vote on the Second Memorandum, February 2012

At the beginning of 2012, Papademos, having previously reached an agreement with the leaders of the parties in his cabinet, negotiated the terms of a major restructuring of the Greek debt, which involved a face value write-down of 53 per cent through private sector involvement (PSI). The *troika*, however, did not trust the commitment of the Greek government to stick to the conditionality that accompanied the memorandum and requested a new agreement to be put to a parliamentary vote. This 'second memorandum' stipulated severe budget cuts and tax hike, and, when the details were leaked to the press, two PASOK and all LAOS members of the cabinet resigned. The latter orchestrated the quick exit after spending less than two months in office, when it became clear that the cost of incumbency was far greater than initially expected. This was particularly true when the opinion polls suggested that the racist party Golden Dawn (XA) had emerged as a serious competitor on issues surrounding immigration and nationalism (Ellinas, 2013), thus threatening the electoral survival of LAOS.

The vote for the second memorandum in February 2012 presented once again voting instructions that tested the limits of party discipline. Both PASOK and, this time, ND instructed their MPs to vote in favour of the second memorandum. Nevertheless, 22 PASOK MPs and 21 ND MPs voted against the memorandum or abstained (see Table 1). Papandreou and Samaras expelled all 43 of them within minutes of the conclusion of the procedure. Ironically, Samaras expelled his MPs for exactly the opposite reason for which he expelled Bakoyannis two years previously. Karatzaferis instructed his MPs to refrain from going to the parliament but two former LAOS ministers did so and voted in favour. They later resigned their seats and joined ND in a gentleman's agreement that enabled LAOS to replace them with the runners-up in the party ticket. Nine of the MPs expelled from ND joined Kammenos in a new party (Independent Greeks [ANEL]) with a Eurosceptic profile bordering on conspiracy theory. Katseli, who was expelled from PASOK for a second time in four months, led another new party (Social Agreement [SA]) that included a further eight MPs expelled from PASOK. From the remainder of the MPs expelled from PASOK, two joined SYRIZA, six joined the Democratic Left, while Dimaras created his own party (*Arma Politon*, or Panhellenic Citizens Chariot [PCC]) and later negotiated a place on an ANEL ticket.

Most of these splinter parties were tested in the May 2012 parliamentary election, one of the most volatile elections in Europe for the past three decades, with fragmentation and polarisation on all sides of the political spectrum (Dinas & Rori, 2013). Samaras won the election, but despite the 50-seat boost awarded to ND by the electoral system, his party remained 43 seats short of a parliamentary majority (see Table 2). Unaccustomed to the practice of coalition bargaining, Greek politicians necessitated another election in June before a compromise in a three-party coalition government could be reached. The biggest winner in the left

Table 2: May 2012 Parliamentary Election Results

	Vote (%)	Δ 2009–12 (%)	Seats
New Democracy (ND)	18.85	−14.62	108
Coalition of the Radical Left (SYRIZA)	16.79	+12.19	52
Panhellenic Socialist Movement (PASOK)	13.18	−30.74	41
Independent Greeks (ANEL)	10.62	New party	33
Communist Party of Greece (KKE)	8.48	+0.94	26
Golden Dawn (XA)	6.97	+6.68	21
Democratic Left	6.11	New party	19
Ecologist Greens	2.93	+0.40	
Popular Orthodox Rally (LAOS)	2.89	−2.74	
Democratic Alliance (DISY)	2.55	New party	
Recreate Greece!	2.15	New party	
Action/Greek Liberals (LIB)	1.80	New party	
Front of the Greek Anticapitalist Left (ANTARSYA)	1.19	+0.83	
Social Agreement	0.96	New party	

anti-memorandum block was undeniably SYRIZA, which seemed to have gained most of the disaffected PASOK voters. ANEL proved the biggest winner in the right-wing anti-memorandum block, while the election saw the rise of the racist Golden Dawn. As expected, the incumbent PASOK took the biggest hit, while the indecisive strategy of Karatzaferis led voters to punish LAOS and end its parliamentary representation. Similarly, the Ecologist Greens' lack of parliamentary representation reduced them to mere spectators of the political developments and prevented them from benefiting from the ensuing electoral volatility. The three liberal parties (Democratic Alliance, Drassi/Greek Liberals, and Recreate Greece!) also fell short of the 3 per cent threshold.

Discussion

The impact of the economic crisis on Greece has certainly had far-reaching political implications. This contribution has sought to pursue some of these implications. Starting with a brief introduction to the events that led to the adoption of the bailout agreement with the EU/IMF/ECB *troika*, it has given an overview of the characteristics of the Greek party system and dimensions of party competition between 1981 and 2010 and presented a narrative of legislative voting during the period 2010–12.

The narrative has pointed out that the advent of the economic crisis in Greece failed to foster greater cooperation among the established political parties that have dominated the political scene since 1981. In contrast to other southern European countries, such as Italy and Portugal, Greek political elites failed to achieve a consensus in dealing with the important impact of the economic crisis. PASOK was the only party to play on the 'responsible party' image (Mair, 2013) when it supported the first bailout package and the midterm plan, even though Prime Minister Papandreou was often challenged by cadres in his own party claiming to represent the interests of the people. Consensus politics emerged only during the talks to form a coalition government, but these only started after the EU put pressure on the political parties, especially ND, in order to enact an emergency funding package. Moreover, the few political actors who supported the government soon found that their choice in doing so had several negative consequences. The dissenting MPs from ND who supported the government bills were expelled from their party. When Samaras changed his stance and supported the government coalition and the second memorandum, he faced a full-blown rebellion from his MPs. Similarly, LAOS, which tactically supported the government, not only lost two of its most prominent cadres to ND, but also lost its parliamentary representation in the subsequent election.

It is interesting to note that each actor's support for government was followed by an increase in fragmentation of the party system, which eventually led to an unprecedented increase in electoral volatility. The expulsion or resignations of MPs who went against their party's voting instructions led to the creation of no less than three splinter parties, which commanded about 14 per cent of the vote in the subsequent election. The effective number of parties (Laakso & Taagepera, 1979) nearly doubled from around 2.5 throughout the period 1981–2010 to 4.17 by April 2012, while the May 2012 election yielded nearly five effective parties at the legislative level and almost nine at the electoral level. Moreover, volatility in the same election reached an all-time high of 48.3 per cent (or 34.1 per cent if we disregard the effect of splinter parties). Although much of the change in the party system and electoral volatility can be explained by the events surrounding legislative voting presented here, the critical outcome of the May 2012 election necessitates a reassessment of the impact of Europe on national party systems.

In a seminal contribution, Mair (2000) argued that the impact of Europe (for Europe read EU) on the national party system had been extremely limited in terms of both party system format (changes in the number of relevant parties) and mechanics (changes in the dimensions of party competition). Mair's conclusion was warranted in view of the empirical evidence that pointed to the lack of Eurosceptic parties that could have managed to mobilise the electorate in first-order national elections, and the lack of salience of the issue of European integration in party competition at the national level. As Mair (2013) observed more recently, however, the economic crisis brought to the forefront the pressure and demands of supranational institutions that play an increasingly important role in national policymaking.

First, the economic crisis triggered a link between Europe and the party system in Greece by blurring the distinction between what Mair (2000) calls 'key European issues' and 'everyday policy questions' (p. 28). If anything, the economic crisis showed that, at least for the eurozone countries, a sharp distinction between the two sets of issues may no longer be valid. Members of the eurozone are 'locked' in an ever-closer Union in which supranational issues such as the future of the common currency are inexorably linked with their day-to-day economic transactions. To this end, Figure 3 presents data from an expert survey conducted in December 2011 (Gemenis & Nezi, 2012), which shows how party positions on both the economic dimension (where higher scores indicate support for the free market versus state intervention), and the memorandum dimension (where higher scores indicate that the party is in favour of a solution for the Greek debt/deficit within the IMF/EU framework) are closely aligned with their positions on European integration.[3] Consequently, this link could awaken the dormant potential of electoral choice based on issues surrounding European integration (De Vries, 2007; Dinas & Pardos-Prado, 2012; Van der Eijk & Franklin, 2007). This awakening may not necessarily take place as a result of European integration issues becoming salient in the national arena, but by virtue of the association of these issues with other (economic) issues that are already considered to be highly salient.

Second, with regard to the channel of influence, Mair (2000) argued that the 'absence of a genuine European party system serves to inhibit any restructuring of domestic party competition that might result from competition at the European level' (p. 28). Once again, the case of Greece points to a different channel of influence. Although it is true that political parties at the national level are not subject to the adaptational pressures faced by member states (Ladrech, 2002, p. 395), the political groups of the EP can often exert significant influence on policy orientation, as has been suggested for parties in central and eastern Europe (Enyedi & Lewis, 2007, pp. 235–239). As argued in the previous section, Samaras's U-turn from opposing to supporting the memorandum can be, at least partially, attributed to the EPP's pressure. In effect, this pressure not only changed the policy direction of what turned out to be the largest party in the 2012 election, but also opened the way for the creation of the splinter ANEL that resented this change of direction.

Figure 3: Party Positions during the Papademos Coalition Government

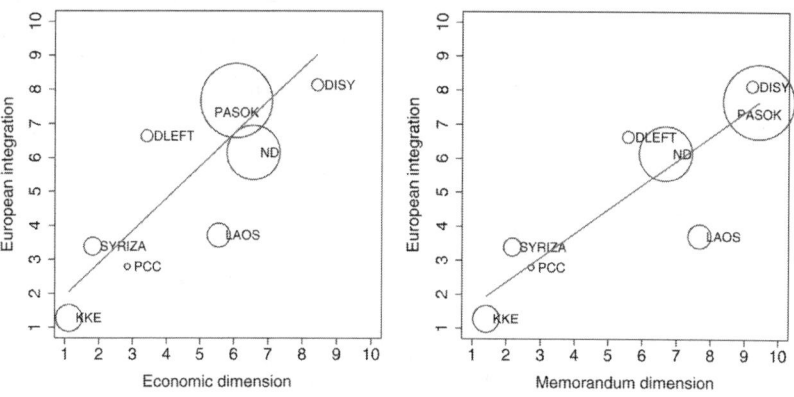

Notes: Size of circles indicates legislative strength; fit line weighted by legislative strength.

Third, although Mair (2000) focused on the possibility of the creation of parties that set themselves against the deepening of European integration, this does not preclude the creation of parties that are supportive of European integration. The EU's austerity response to the economic crisis may have led parties that were otherwise reasonably supportive of European integration towards a more Eurosceptic stance, prompting the creation of pro-EU parties. As argued earlier, the creation of the Democratic Left party was partially a response to internal conflict over the party organisation structure, but also partly a response to SYRIZA's trajectory towards Euroscepticism.

In short, this contribution illustrates how the Greek parliament failed to experience a consensus between government and opposition, as elsewhere in southern Europe. Rather than fostering cooperation and consensus, the economic crisis opened the way for new mechanisms and channels for the impact of Europe on national politics and widened the rift between the responsive and responsible aspects of representative government (Mair, 2013). Those political actors who claimed to represent their constituents were at odds with those who claimed that they could deliver a viable solution to the crisis. As the case of ND has shown, fence-sitting was not a viable option. The pressure from Europe was such that government parties were pushed towards a 'responsible' conceptualisation of government claiming that they could deliver a way out of the crisis, at odds with their representative function. As they could no longer claim to represent their constituents, fragmentation gave way to polarisation, volatility, and the eventual collapse of the long-established party system.

Notes

1. For instance, when PASOK realised that changing the electoral system would prevent ND from forming a government, it collaborated with the left parties to change the system to proportional representation. ND was then forced to form, essentially, a caretaker coalition with the left and when it later secured a parliamentary majority, changed the system to the less proportional and introduced a 3 per cent threshold for parliamentary representation in 1993. Most recently, PASOK introduced a 40 (out of 300) seat bonus for the first party, which was quickly changed to 50 when ND won the next election (Gemenis, 2008, pp. 95–96, 100).
2. Expert surveys have often been criticised in terms of their ability to portray parties' positions accurately (see Steenbergen & Marks, 2007). More specifically, the experts' own political preferences may induce them to place certain parties towards the extremes, whereas their imperfect expertise

can lead to measurement error and a centrist bias in the estimates. Although we do not have the means of assessing the impact of experts' political preferences on their judgements in the Chapel Hill Expert Surveys, the examination of a survey on political parties in Greece showed such bias to be minimal (Gemenis & Nezi, 2012). Moreover, the perceptual agreement among the Greek experts in the expert surveys used here is generally high, save a few expected exceptions (see Table A1 in the Appendix). We contend that these problems are not serious enough to alter the inferences made in this paper, especially when compared with the readily available but highly implausible manifesto-based content analysis estimates for Greek parties (Dinas & Gemenis, 2010).

3. As in the previous figures, higher values indicate support for further European integration. Even though the party system at the time included parties that would become electorally successful in the following months, the figure is restricted to those having parliamentary representation in December 2011.

References

Antonis Samaras stunned Europe with his intransigence. (2011). Retrieved from http://www.grreporter.info/en/antonis_samaras_stunned_europe_his_intransigence/4734

Bakker, R., de Vries, C., Edwards, E., Hooghe, L., Jolly, S., Marks, G., ... Vachudova, A. M. (2012). Measuring party positions in Europe: The Chapel Hill Expert Survey trend file, 1999–2010. *Party Politics*. Advance online publication. doi:10.1177/1354068812462931

Close, D. (2009). The New Democracy government and the continuing struggle for modernisation, 2004–2007. In D. Close (Ed.), *Proceedings of the Biennial International Conference of Greek Studies* (pp. 283–292). Adelaide: Flinders University Press.

De Vries, C. E. (2007). Sleeping giant: Fact or fairytale? How European integration affects national elections. *European Union Politics*, *8*, 363–385.

Dinas, E. (2010). The Greek general election of 2009: PASOK – the third generation. *West European Politics*, *33*, 389–398.

Dinas, E., & Gemenis, K. (2010). Measuring parties' ideological positions with manifesto data: A critical evaluation of the competing methods. *Party Politics*, *16*, 427–450.

Dinas, E., & Pardos-Prado, S. (2012). A hidden giant? Exploring the centrifugal dynamics of attitudes towards the European unification. *Acta Politica*, *47*, 378–399.

Dinas, E., & Rori, L. (2013). The 2012 Greek parliamentary elections: Fear and loathing in the polls. *West European Politics*, *36*, 270–282.

Ellinas, A. A. (2013). The rise of Golden Dawn: The new face of the far right in Greece. *South European Society & Politics*, *18*, 543–565.

Enyedi, Z., & Lewis, P. G. (2007). The impact of the European Union on party politics in central and eastern Europe. In P. G. Lewis & Z. Mansfeldova (Eds.), *The European Union and party politics in east central Europe* (pp. 231–249). Basingstoke: Palgrave Macmillan.

Featherstone, K. (2005). Introduction: 'Modernisation' and the structural constraints of Greek politics. *West European Politics*, *28*, 223–241.

Gemenis, K. (2008). The 2007 parliamentary election in Greece. *Mediterranean Politics*, *13*, 95–101.

Gemenis, K. (2009). A Green comeback in Greece? The Ecologist Greens in the 2007 parliamentary election. *Environmental Politics*, *18*, 128–134.

Gemenis, K. (2010). Winning votes and weathering storms: The 2009 European and parliamentary elections in Greece. *Representation*, *46*, 353–362.

Gemenis, K. (2012). The 2010 regional elections in Greece: Voting for regional governance or protesting the IMF? *Regional & Federal Studies*, *22*, 107–115.

Gemenis, K., & Dinas, E. (2010). Confrontation still? Examining parties' policy positions in Greece. *Comparative European Politics*, *8*, 179–201.

Gemenis, K., & Nezi, R. (2012). *The 2011 political parties expert survey in Greece* [Data set]. Data Archiving and Networked Services. Persistent identifier: urn: nbn:nl:ui:13-a9zi-p9.

Hooghe, L., & Marks, G. (2008). A postfunctionalist theory of European integration: From permissive consensus to constraining dissensus. *British Journal of Political Science*, *39*, 1–23.

Hooghe, L., Marks, G., & Wilson, C. (2002). Does left/right structure party positions on European integration? *Comparative Political Studies*, *35*, 973–976.

Kalyvas, S. N. (1997). Polarization in Greek politics: PASOK's first four years, 1981–1985. *Journal of the Hellenic Diaspora*, *23*, 83–104.

Katz, R. S., & Mair, P. (1995). Changing models of party organization and party democracy: The emergence of the cartel party. *Party Politics*, *1*, 5–28.

Laakso, M., & Taagepera, R. (1979). Effective number of parties: A measure with application to West Europe. *Comparative Political Studies*, *12*, 3–27.

Ladrech, R. (2002). Europeanization and political parties: Towards a framework for analysis. *Party Politics*, *8*, 389–403.

Lyrintzis, C. (2005). The changing party system: Stable democracy, contested 'modernisation'. *West European Politics*, *28*, 242–259.

Mair, P. (2000). The limited impact of Europe on national party systems. *West European Politics*, *23*(4), 27–51.

Mair, P. (2013). Smaghi versus the parties: Representative government and institutional constraints. In W. Streeck & A. Schäfer (Eds.), *Politics in the age of austerity* (pp. 143–168). Cambridge: Polity Press.

Mavrogordatos, G. Th. (1997). From traditional clientilism to machine politics: The impact of PASOK populism in Greece. *South European Society & Politics*, *2*(3), 1–26.

Nezi, R. (2012). Economic voting under the economic crisis: Evidence from Greece. *Electoral Studies*, *31*, 498–505.

Nezi, R., Sotiropoulos, D. A., & Toka, P. (2010). Attitudes of Greek parliamentarians towards European and national identity, representation and scope of governance. *South European Society & Politics*, *15*, 79–96.

Nicolacopoulos, I. (2005). Elections and voters, 1974–2004: Old cleavages and new issues. *West European Politics*, *28*, 260–278.

Papatheodorou, F., & Machin, D. (2003). The umbilical cord that was never cut: The post-dictatorial intimacy between the political elite and the mass media in Greece and Spain. *European Journal of Communication*, *18*, 31–54.

Pappas, T. S. (2003). The transformation of the Greek party system since 1951. *West European Politics*, *26*(2), 90–114.

Pappas, T. S. (2009). Patrons against partisans: The politics of patronage in mass ideological parties. *Party Politics*, *15*, 315–334.

Pappas, T. S. (2010). Macroeconomic policy, strategic leadership, and voter behaviour: The disparate tales of socialist reformism in Greece and Spain during the 1980s. *West European Politics*, *33*, 1241–1260.

Pappas, T. S., & Assimakopoulou, Z. (2012). Party patronage in Greece: Political entrepreneurship in a party patronage democracy. In P. Kopecky, P. Mair, & M. Spirova (Eds.), *Party patronage and party governments in European democracies* (pp. 144–162). Oxford: Oxford University Press.

Pappas, T. S., & Dinas, E. (2006). From opposition to power: Greek conservatism reinvented. *South European Society & Politics*, *11*, 473–493.

Sotiropoulos, D. A. (2012). A democracy under stress: Greece since 2010. *Taiwan Journal of Democracy*, *8*, 27–49.

Steenbergen, M., & Marks, G. (2007). Evaluating expert judgements. *European Journal of Political Research*, *46*, 347–366.

Teperoglou, E., & Tsatsanis, E. (2011). A new divide? The impact of globalisation on national party systems. *West European Politics*, *34*, 1207–1228.

Tsarouhas, D. (2012). The political origins of the Greek crisis: Domestic failures and the EU factor. *Insight Turkey*, *14*(2), 83–98.

Van der Eijk, C. (2001). Measuring agreement in ordered rating scales. *Quality & Quantity*, *35*, 325–341.

Van der Eijk, C., & Franklin, M. (2007). The sleeping giant: Potential for political mobilization of disaffection with European integration. In W. van der Brug & C. van der Eijk (Eds.), *European elections and domestic politics: Lessons from the past and scenarios for the future* (pp. 189–208). South Bend, IN: University of Notre Dame Press.

Van Versendaal, H. (2011). The wrong mix that pushed ND to the right. *Kathimerini*. Retrieved from http://www.ekathimerini.com/4dcgi/_w_articles_wsite3_1_20/10/2011_411252

Vasilopoulou, S. (2011). Europe integration and the radical right: Three patterns of opposition. *Government and Opposition*, *46*, 223–244.

Verney, S. (2011). An exceptional case? Party and popular Euroscepticism in Greece, 1959–2009. *South European Society & Politics*, *16*, 51–79.

Appendix

Table A1: Perceptual Agreement among Experts in the Chapel Hill Expert Surveys (1999–2010)

	1999				2002				2006				2010			
	Econ.	Soc.	L-R	EU	Econ.	Soc.	L-R	EU	Econ.	Soc.	L-R	EU	Econ.	Soc.	L-R	EU
PASOK	0.56	0.83	0.62	1	0.78	0.71	0.91	0.93	0.73	0.78	0.91	0.93	0.66	0.73	0.8	0.74
ND	0.8	0.69	0.68	0.9	0.76	0.74	0.86	0.83	0.82	0.72	0.91	0.89	0.69	0.7	0.84	0.69
SYN/SYRIZA	0.91	0.68	0.62	0.36	0.82	0.87	0.92	1	0.84	0.68	0.91	0.59	0.78	0.63	0.78	0.96
KKE	0.83	0.57	0.89	1	0.88	0.25	0.9	0.9	0.98	0.32	0.96	1	0.98	0.27	0.93	1
POLAN	0.74	0.56	0.8	0.67												
DIKKI	0.77	0.74	0.71	0.61												
LAOS									0.46	0.93	0.84	0.34	0.47	0.91	0.91	0.67
Eco.Greens													0.75	0.88	0.92	0.8

Source: Entries are Van der Eijk's (2001) agreement coefficient A.

Table A2: Chronicle of Events, November 2009–May 2012

Date	Description of Event
5 November 2009	Prime Minister George Papandreou raises his government's estimates for Greece's budget deficit for 2009 from 5 to 12.7 per cent
2 February 2010	Papandreou announces in a televised address the need for austerity measures and appeals for support
23 April 2010	Prime Minister Papandreou announces in a televised address that Greece has requested international funds to avoid bankruptcy
2 May 2010	The Eurogroup agrees to provide bilateral loans to Greece in a joint package with the IMF
6 May 2010	The Greek parliament passes first austerity bill
7 November 2010	The first round of local and regional elections takes places. The second round, whenever one is needed, takes place a week later
25 May 2011	The Greek *indignados* occupy Syntagma Square in front of the parliament
29 June 2011	The Greek parliament approves the midterm fiscal plan
31 October 2011	Papandreou calls for a referendum on the IMF/EU bailout package
3 November 2011	Papandreou calls off the referendum after narrowly winning a vote of no confidence in the parliament
10 November 2011	Papandreou steps down and the party leaders of PASOK, ND, and LAOS agree to give Lucas Papademos, a former central banker, the mandate to form an interim coalition government
12 February 2012	The Greek parliament passes the second austerity bill
11 April 2012	Papademos asks President Karolos Papoulias to dissolve the parliament, and elections announced for 6 May
6 May 2012	The first parliamentary election since the start of the debt crisis takes place. The three top-ranking parties take turns in leading coalition formation talks but fail to form a government coalition. Papoulias calls a new election for 17 June

From a Technocratic Solution to a Fragile *Grand Coalition*: The Impact of the Economic Crisis on Parliamentary Government in Italy

FRANCESCO MARANGONI and
LUCA VERZICHELLI

Italy is an interesting case to be included in a comparative analysis of the effects determined by the recent financial crisis on the European political systems, because of the distinctiveness characterising the recent development of this parliamentary democracy. The processes of making and breaking governments, in particular, have been particularly unusual: the end of the governmental experience of Silvio Berlusconi and the formation of the technical government led by Mario Monti have been strongly influenced by external factors, as well as the recent formation of the government guided by Enrico Letta, supported by a broad coalition including the former competing centre-right and centre-left cartels. The paper focuses on the practices of executive–legislative relationships in Italy between 2008 and the 2013 elections. Its basic puzzle is to understand the effective impact determined by the economic crisis over the core mechanisms of parliamentary democracy. Comparing the impact of the governmental policy agenda set by the technocratic cabinet vis-à-vis the previous 'political' executives, and measuring the reactions of the different parliamentary actors, it is possible to test a number of empirical propositions concerning the transformation of the adversarial mode that emerged in past years into a more or less consensual parliamentary atmosphere.

Introduction

There can be no doubt that the Italian political system has been deeply affected by the recent economic crisis: the unresolved problems of a difficult democracy, one that is constantly caught between attempted adjustments and inertia, have resurfaced dramatically, and the European Central Bank (EBC) and other supranational institutions have called for the introduction of a number of measures to anchor the country to the eurozone. Although we do not intend to return to the theme of *Italian exceptionality*, we cannot examine the relationship between economic crisis and modes of parliamentary opposition without introducing a caveat regarding the distinctiveness of the Italian case study, for two reasons.

At first, contrary to what happened in other countries, the crucial decisions taken in order to cope with the crisis were not taken by an electorally legitimated government, but by a new 'technocratic' government. The period examined here is basically that of the executive led by Mario Monti, and supported by a broad coalition of all major parliamentary parties. In a sense, we could say that the 'inclusion' of the opposition in the (technocratic) government majority is the main political outcome of the economic crisis in Italy.

Second, the timing of the economic crisis has overlapped with a difficult phase of political transition characterised by an increasing lack of legitimacy, and by the decline of several of those political actors who had consolidated their positions over the last two decades. The institutional crisis reached its peak with the crisis of the fourth Berlusconi government and the formation of the Monti government (Fusaro, 2012), a technocratic solution in which Italy's European partners and the president of the Republic played a crucial role. In this regard, therefore, the transformation of Italian parliamentarianism between 2011 and 2013 was not so much a process of increasing cooperation between majority and opposition bodies, as a complicated transitional process involving the dismantling of the adversarial parliamentary model that had emerged over the previous two decades, and a very uncertain phase of leadership turnover.

We could argue that the impossibility of moving towards a more *consensual form of decision-making* within a context of constant political competition is due to the structural constraints at work in Italian politics (Fabbrini, 2013). Additional political conditions include the consolidated degree of polarisation of legislative behaviours in fields such as budgetary and macroeconomic reform (Giuliani, 2008), together with the development, over the years, of a sort of 'ideological' anti-European view in certain minority (albeit pivotal) centre-right parties (Conti & Memoli, 2014).

The range of hypotheses we can define to explain the peculiar reaction of Italy's parliamentary democracy to the crisis is therefore rather broad. In order to disentangle this complicated interplay of factors and actors, we argue that the fragility of the political context, and in particular the weakened position of the major partisan actors during the immediate phase of *mandatory responses*, has played a crucial role. Moreover, we shall also take account of the return of certain parties to a pure 'opposition mode', due to their clear anti-European stance.

In sum, we propose an in-depth analysis of the executive–legislative relationship during the XVI legislature, arguing that the strategies of partisan actors could have changed significantly during this period, not only in terms of policy preferences, but also in terms of prioritising mandatory policy measures, daily bargaining and flagship partisan issues. Unlike other country studies, therefore, we shall not be covering extensively cohesion within those parties constituting the slender opposition to the Monti government, given their political isolation during the final phase of the legislature. On the contrary, we are more interested in assessing the internal cohesion within the large tripartite coalition sustaining the technocratic cabinet, and in measuring the changing attitudes of these actors during the transition from the adversarial phase of the fourth Berlusconi government to the technocratic phase.

The following section introduces readers to the political scenario that evolved between 2008 and 2012, that is, from the apparent consolidation of a majoritarian model, to the failure of this approach with the crisis of the fourth Berlusconi government and the formation of Mario Monti's technocratic government. The subsequent section offers a few general propositions to be tested empirically. We then analyse the changes in parliamentary dynamics, focusing on the nature of delegation to the technocratic government, the role of governmental leadership, and the development of legislative behaviour. Finally, we return to the general question of the relationship between the crisis and the suspension of the 'adversarial mode', and we discuss the principal implications that can be drawn from this analysis.

Italian Parliamentary Democracy and the Failure of the 'Majoritarian Turn' (2008–12)

When the Italian Republic's XVI legislature began (April 2008), many indicators seemed to point to the end of a long period of political transition and the start of a new era of majoritarian democracy. After the failure of the centre-left coalition led by Romano Prodi, and the early dissolution of the parliament after less than two years, the right-wing coalition had won the elections and the fourth Berlusconi cabinet could be formed, supported by a large political majority. Moreover, the new majority was made up of just two parties: the People of Freedom Party (PDL), resulting from a merger between Berlusconi's *Forza Italia* and Fini's National Alliance (*Alleanza Nazionale*), and the Northern League (LN). On the other hand, only three parties constituted the parliamentary opposition to the right-wing government: the largest of these was the newly founded *Partito Democratico* (PD), the result of a merger between the principal heirs of the communist party (the *Left democrats*) and the progressive Christian Democrats of *La Margherita* (the Daisy). Two smaller parliamentary groups consisted of the IdV (*Italia dei Valori* – the Italy of Values Party), the movement founded by former 'clean hands' prosecutor Antonio Di Pietro, whose principal goal was the moralisation of political life, and the Centrist Union (UDC) led by a former ally of Berlusconi, Pier Ferdinando Casini.

This simplification of the political scenario was the consequence of the strategies adopted by the two largest parties (the PDL and PD), whose leaderships had argued that it was time to implement their 'majoritarian mission'. Indeed, after the implosion of the composite centre-left coalition supporting the Prodi government, the newly founded party dominating that particular area of the political spectrum (the PD) decided to run alone,[1] although this was probably what led to its electoral defeat. At the same time, Silvio Berlusconi, strengthened by a new tide of personal support, was able to merge the largest centre-right parties,[2] thus paving the way for the official creation of the PDL. The success of the centre-right cartel,[3] together with the excellent results obtained by the PD's candidates, was reflected in the weakening of the minor parties at both ends of the political spectrum, most of which were excluded from participation in the new parliament. The number of parliamentary parties thus fell to its lowest level ever in the history of the Italian Republic, with the LN (on the right) and the IdV (on the left) constituting the only possible coalition partners of the PDL and the PD, respectively (Chiaramonte, 2010).

The 'majoritarian' parliament, however, had a very short life. The reasons underlying the progressive return to a fragmented political scenario are to be found in the persisting uncertainties within the Italian party system. Indeed, three important phenomena witnessed during the legislature should be mentioned here. The first of these is represented by the internal problems of the main governing party, the PDL, which had already emerged in 2010, when the party's second most important figure – the former president of the right-wing *Alleanza Nazionale*, Gianfranco Fini – decided to create a new movement (Future and Liberty for Italy [FLI]) and to move to the opposition benches. However, Fini's attempt to reunite his former colleagues from *Alleanza Nazionale*, thus forcing a breakdown in Berlusconi's leadership, failed: Berlusconi won a dramatic parliamentary confidence vote, albeit by a weakened majority, on 16 December 2010 in the lower chamber.

The second phenomenon concerns the internal problems within the PD, which led to the party losing a small, but significant, number of parliamentarians during the course of the legislature. They included the former leader of the Daisy, Francesco Rutelli, who joined the centrist alliance with a handful of other moderate MPs. Further manoeuvres characterised the left-wing fringes of the parliamentary group: despite its exclusion from parliament, the so-called 'radical left' was reorganised by a new leader, the Chief Executive of the Puglia Regional Government Nichi Vendola, who became the leader of a new left-wing movement (*Sinistra e Libertà* [SeL]) whose candidates managed to defeat local PD leaders in several towns and cities, including the important municipality of Milan, where a SeL candidate – Giuliano Pisapia – won the primary election and was subsequently elected mayor in the spring of 2011.

Finally, a general anti-party sentiment had re-emerged, encouraged by repeated cases of political corruption and maladministration (Vannucci, 2009). During the course of the legislature, popular distrust of the governing classes was increasingly evident, and in the spring of 2012 this feeling materialised in the form of strong support for the Five Stars Movement (*Movimento Cinque Stelle*) founded a few years before by the former TV comedian Beppe Grillo. This result was a foretaste of the extraordinary success of this new political movement in the February 2013 general election.

The political turmoil characterising the XVI legislature is, however, clearly connected to the global economic situation and to the European scenario: one should remember here that the collapse of the fourth Berlusconi government (November 2011) was ultimately due not to any no confidence parliamentary vote, but to a political compromise largely inspired by Italy's European partners and diplomatically managed by the president of the Republic, Giorgio

Napolitano. Likewise, the European institutions – the Central Bank and the European Commission above all – supported the adoption of strict economic measures in order to cope with the dramatic economic situation, and encouraged the formation of a technocratic government led by the former EU commissioner, Mario Monti.

Moreover, debate over the financial crisis clearly saw the 'European issue' back on the public agenda: while there was a broad (albeit extremely fragile) consensus among the main parliamentary parties regarding the introduction of a number of strict measures, and support for the Monti government, the radical left and the far-right (neo-liberal conservatives and the Northern League MPs) often resorted to anti-economic and monetary union rhetoric, sometimes expressing the ultimate idea of doing away with the euro and returning to a system of national currencies. Unlike during the first decade of this century, when the positions of the two rival governing coalitions were significantly polarised on specific policies, but displayed no real questioning of their *being European* (Conti, 2009), the issue of European integration (and the complex aspects thereof) once again became significantly divisive. The classic pattern of polarisation between mainstream and fringe European parties re-emerged, although a confusing number of positions were also present within the parties themselves (in particular within the PDL).

Hence, the attempt at implementing a 'Westminster turn' in Italian politics was rejected owing to certain specific political conditions, including the fragmentation of the party system and the weakness of the new partisan organisations, although exogenous factors, and in particular the implications of the economic crisis and the consequent pressure from the EU's institutions, also played an important part. The chosen way out of the stalemate brought on by the failure of the fourth Berlusconi government was a 'technocratic' government supported by the main parties on both sides of the party-political spectrum. Although this was not the only case of a technocratic government being formed to cope with an emergency situation,[4] the Italian experience seems a unique example of the separation of responsibility from representation (Mair, 2011).

Refining our Empirical Propositions

This last consideration leads us directly to the crucially important question we wish to investigate here. In theory at least, at such a time of economic crisis Italy could not have afforded the creation of a technical government based on a pure model of party abdication (Pasquino & Valbruzzi, 2012): a rational sense of responsibility on the part of the major parties would have led them to limit their responsiveness towards their respective constituencies, while sharing the cost of the mandatory responses adopted within a broad cross-party coalition. In practice, however, the technocratic solution can be seen as a partial form of party abdication, to be employed at a particular stage of the emergency: a sort of intermediation between parliamentary principals and the governmental agent, designed to raise institutional responsibility. Therefore, the degree of party delegation to the (technocratic) executive has to be investigated and measured in an empirical manner.

The partial abdication of partisan prerogatives can therefore be seen not so much as a lessening of the strategic polarisation between the main parties, as a limitation of room for the 'usual bargaining' and, above all, as the suspension of partisan flagship issues, during a phase in which the reputation of all political actors was at an all-time low.

Certain logical objections may, however, be made to application of the party abdication model: a first objection concerns full policy delegation to the technical government when the executive's proposals clash with the 'core preferences' of a given party. For example, centre-left members of the majority will be less inclined to support welfare reductions, while, on the other hand, centre-right members of the majority will oppose any governmental proposal for the implementation of new property taxes. In other words, what is being discussed here is the government's capacity to set an agenda consisting of its own priorities – a capacity that should not be taken for granted, given the extreme heterogeneity of the coalition upon which such government relies, but one that is of crucial importance at such a delicate moment in time. A technocratic government might introduce original solutions within the narrow confines of its technical mandate, but in general we should expect it to follow an 'adaptive' approach with regard to the rest of the items on its agenda. That is not to say that the executive avoids making decisions of which a given coalition partner would disapprove: this would imply no party abdication at all (and possibly no policy action). On the contrary, it is more likely to formulate its own working agenda as a combination of measures alternatively 'detrimental' (as far as parties' traditional constituencies and policy commitments are concerned) and 'beneficial' to both camps.

A second type of restriction on governmental policy delegation concerns the established attitudes of different party elites towards European commitments: the legislative behaviour of those MPs from truly 'core European' parties who are more likely to cooperate with, rather than rebel against, government actions designed to meet 'European constraints'. From this point of view, a clear difference between the broad Europeanism of the centre-left (especially in the XVI legislature, when the radical left was excluded from parliament) and the more composite Europeanism of the centre-right is foreseeable, given the findings of previous analyses (Roux & Verzichelli, 2010).

In the Italian case, if what we have just argued about the impact of pro- (or anti-) European attitudes, leaders' capability and party control over parliamentary groups is true, we would expect the PD and above all those MPs to the centre of the political spectrum to be more supportive of the measures negotiated by Mario Monti with Italy's European partners. The more sceptical (individual) members of the former centre-right alliance, on the contrary, will be more inclined to follow the Northern League in opposing the decisions of Monti's technocratic government. Owing to the critical juncture in Berlusconi's leadership, and the divisions within the PDL, the interruption to the process of institutionalisation of this parliamentary party will have led to greater disloyalty among its MPs (that is, a reduced degree of party unity when it comes to supporting the techno-cratic government's decisions).

Party Abdication in Prioritising Issues and Formulating Policies

During the rapid formation of his government, Monti often appealed to the notion of 'national obligation' (Marangoni, 2012), which was also a frequently used catchword in the programme he presented to parliament. This concept explicitly refers to the narrow scope of his government: the mandate demanded of parlia-ment was indeed limited to those actions to be taken in order to deal with the economic emergency and to keep Italy within the eurozone. In order to achieve this goal, Monti formed an 'interim government' staffed by people from outside the political sphere, even at the junior ministerial level (Verzichelli & Cotta, 2013).

However, a limited mandate in terms of both policy issues and policymakers within the cabinet does not necessarily mean a weak agenda: given the magnitude of the crisis, the cabinet was able to use all the 'preferential procedures' provided for by parliamentary rules on governmental action, and above all it could force legislators to intervene in other policy areas that were not supposed to be directly affected by 'governmental pledges'. Such policy actions included, for instance, the institutional arrangements to reduce the cost of politics, and the reform of local government administration, of public funding of political parties, and of Italy's electoral system. Therefore, it is important to examine how the new execu-tive renewed the list of priorities, and to understand to what extent the mandate given to Mario Monti's technocratic leadership was limited, compared with the room for manoeuvre previously afforded to Silvio Berlusconi.

During the course of his speech to parliament outlining the technocratic gov-ernment's programme, Monti identified two primary objectives: (1) the guaran-teed sustainability of public finances; and (2) implementation of a plan for development, modernisation and growth. The prime minister then outlined the main strategies he had in mind for achieving these objectives. Said strategies con-sisted of: the improvement of public finances; the implementation of pledges given to the EU; the reduction in the cost of maintaining elected bodies; the rationalisation of the public administration; the reform of welfare legislation; measures designed to counter tax evasion; the taxation of property; the selling off of publicly owned real estate; a series of macroeconomic policies designed to encourage intervention in the labour market; and a series of microeconomic policies designed to encourage growth.

Drawing upon an analytical framework widely referred to in the literature (Moury, 2012; Moury & Timmermans, 2008; Royed, 1996), we can indeed provide a more detailed and systematic analysis of the prime minister's

Table 1: The Monti Government's Programmatic Pledges by Areas of Action

Area of Action	No. of Real Pledges	%
Improvement in public finances	2	7.41
Implementation of the pledges made to the EU	2	7.41
Reduction in the costs of maintaining elected bodies	2	7.41
Rationalisation of the public administration	5	18.52
Reform of welfare legislation	0	0.00
The fight against tax evasion	2	7.41
The taxation of property	1	3.70
The selling off of publicly owned real estate	2	7.41
Macroeconomic policies to encourage growth	3	11.11
Intervention in the labour market	4	14.81
Microeconomic policies to encourage growth	4	14.81
Total:	27	100.00

programmatic speech. First, we shall break the speech down into individual items (complete sentences) and identify those that represent concrete objectives to be pursued (for example, 'proceed to amalgamate the agencies of social security'), while distinguishing them from those of a purely symbolic nature (for example, 'fight crime') and those useful for developing themes of a more general character (for example, 'Europe is living through a more difficult period than at any time since the war'). Textual analysis of Monti's programmatic speech produces 27 items classifiable as concrete pledges. Table 1 shows how these pledges are distributed over 10 different policy areas.

The aim of rationalising the public administration is the most detailed one (five pledges, 18 per cent of the total), while the reform of welfare rules (which was nevertheless among the first, and most important, acts of the technocratic government) appears somewhat marginal within the context of the prime minister's speech. Indeed, looking at these 'policy horizons', one might say that Monti's pledges were simply the reformulation of an existing agenda of 'mandatory actions': in the end, the debt crisis and the stagnation of the national economy have always been the main concerns of any government during the history of Italy's Second Republic. However, the severe emergency in which Monti found himself operating certainly called for a strong commitment to establishing, in a much more open and direct manner than in the recent past, a plan for structural reforms that would probably not have elicited the support of a 'political' cabinet (Fabbrini, 2013). Thus, almost 1000 words (about one-quarter of the whole speech) directly concerned the reduction of public debt and the respective actions to be taken in order to achieve this target. The same target was mentioned only briefly by Berlusconi in his 2008 inaugural speech (about 30 words being dedicated to such), which instead was far more concerned with other general themes, such as growth, institutional reform and citizens' security.

The programme established by Monti and his technicians implied a potentially high cost to be paid by political actors in electoral terms, and sparked immediate debate about the possible limitations placed by MPs on the cabinet's actions. The prime minister's need for the support of a large, variegated majority for the executive, therefore, offers an additional key to our reading of the agenda presented by government to parliament. In keeping with the aforementioned 'adaptive agenda' model, rather than presenting a genuinely new agenda, Monti's approach embraced the combination of measures already present in both political camps, by proposing a logic of 'tickets' to be constantly negotiated in order to foster the necessary cooperation among the parliamentary actors (Marangoni, 2012). The reforms of the pension system and the labour market, for instance, were expected to gain most support from the centre-right, while the introduction of a tax on large-scale personal wealth had been proposed by the Democratic Party during its time in opposition. Another example of this logic of tickets was the trade-off between incentives to private investors financing infrastructural projects (following the previous centre-right government's lead) and the reintroduction of the council-levied property tax abolished by that same government, a measure which had been strong opposed by the centre-left.

We could easily argue that the work of the technocratic government was not so much the exercise of positive agenda-setting power in relation to crucially important new issues, but basically that of freezing the most divisive key issues (at this point reduced in number by the hollowed bargaining power of the two leading parliamentary groups) and of transforming other existing issues into forms of 'mandatory action'. However, the definition of the government's agenda is not confined to the government formation stage. The different decision-making arenas (from the cabinet to the Houses of Parliament) are involved in a daily bargaining process that needs to be analysed separately, if we are to confirm those limitations to party delegation we have noted so far.

Legislative Processes in Times of Crisis: Personalised Premierships and Complex Bargaining

The argument that Italy's political parties abdicated from their 'natural' role as mediating bodies in the selection of rulers directly implies, among other things, the rise of a strong 'principal' within the cabinet: a technocratic prime minister is obviously largely free to choose his/her ministers, and the traditional constraints of coalitional portfolio allocation no longer affect the process of governmental formation. Now, there can be no doubt that the Monti government's term in power replicated this situation of prime ministerial dominance: between his inauguration speech of 17 November 2011 and his resignation on 21 December 2012, Monti was the undisputed leader in the legislative process. However, we need to examine the extent to which the super-activity of the technocratic premier changed the nature of the executive–legislative relationship. The aggregate data concerning the impact of governmental bills, presented in Figure 1,[5] do not show any significant difference between the political and technical phases, with the partial exception of the increase in the use of emergency

Figure 1: Percentage Distribution of the Government's Bills and Other Measures by Type of Measure (Excluding Treaty Ratifications)

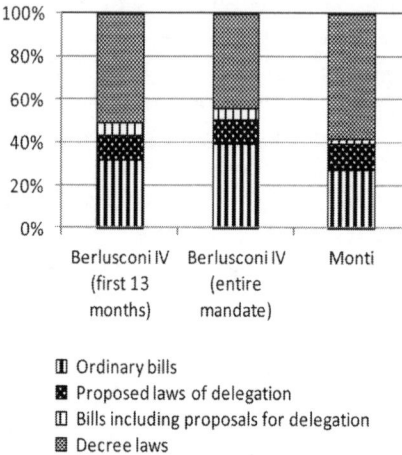

Ordinary bills
Proposed laws of delegation
Bills including proposals for delegation
Decree laws

Source: CIRCaP (www.circap.org).

degrees by the Monti government, which can in any case be accounted for by the financial crisis.

Data for the sponsorship of governmental legislative items show that the technocratic cabinet displayed a very high degree of *personalisation* in terms of the direct involvement of its leader in legislative action. Monti was indeed much more inclined than Berlusconi had been to 'sign' personally legislative bills sponsoring (or co-sponsoring) more than 75 per cent of all legislation promoted by his government (Marangoni, 2013). One should remember that Monti preserved a broad delegation as minister of the economy up until 11 July 2011. Indeed, his degree of autonomy was remarkable, especially when compared with that witnessed during a 'strong' premiership such as that of Berlusconi.

The prime minister's 'signature' on the majority of governmental legislative items is an important indicator of his power to MPs, but is not very clear to the public. On the contrary, change in the nature of the legislative bills submitted by the technocratic, personalised government was represented by the consistency between the government's daily actions and its programmatic platform (Table 2). As one can see, the limited number of bills in the legislative pipeline (together with a substantial number of decrees) emphasises the technocratic role of Monti (and a few of his own ministers), who largely adhered to their original programmatic mandate.[6] In any case, this had a significant impact on the broader executive–legislative relationship: by focusing on a select few, crucially important programmatic issues, the government had the opportunity to lead public debate without calling for too many compromises, or enforcing some sort of parliamentary closure on certain crucial occasions. Indeed, such a strategy was actually

Table 2: Percentage of Government Bills Linked to Programmatic Objectives (Excluding Treaty Ratifications)

Berlusconi IV (First 13 Months)			Berlusconi IV (Entire Mandate)			Monti		
Type of Initiative	No.	%	Type of Initiative	No.	%	Type of Initiative	No.	%
Bills	15	44.1	Bills	21	28.0	Bills	8	34.8
Ord	9	40.9	Ord	14	20.0	Ord	5	33.3
Del	4	50.0	Del	6	28.6	Del	2	28.6
IncDel	2	50.0	IncDel	3	30.0	IncDel	1	100
Decree laws	21	58.3	Decree laws	30	37.5	Decree laws	18	51.4
Total:	36	51.4	Total:	53	29.3	Total:	26	44.8

IncDel = ordinary bills including proposals of delegation.

mentioned by Monti and by some of his ministers. In the next section we are going to examine whether such a strategy was actually successful in sustaining the governmental items within parliament during the government's 13 months of office, compared with the more usual scenario of an 'adversarial' parliamentary regime witnessed during the Second Republic, and in particular during the three years of the centre-right fourth Berlusconi government

The findings and information analysed so far confirm the unique nature of the parliamentary mandate given to the technocratic government during the final period of the XVI legislature: parliament pledged itself to implementing a series of radical, tough measures, albeit limited to certain specific areas of policy-making. The questions to be raised now, therefore, are as follows. To what extent was such a division of labour between government and parliament actually employed during the difficult term in office of the technocratic government? Was the government's interpretation of such a difficult mandate clear to, and undisputed by, all MPs? The answers to these questions will help us decide whether there was any real change towards a broader pattern of parliamentary consensus. A first hint is provided by the remarkable overall success of governmental bills (see Table 3), although this is clearly due to the strategy to guarantee

Table 3: Rate of Success of Government Bills by Type of Bill (Ratifications Excluded)

Berlusconi IV (After 13 Months)			Berlusconi IV (Entire Mandate)			Monti		
Type of Initiative	No.	%	Type of Initiative	No.	%	Type of Initiative	No.	%
Bills	11	32.4	Bills	47	46.5	Bills	5	21.7
Ord	8	36.4	Ord	35	50.0	Ord	3	20.0
Del	2	25.0	Del	7	33.3	Del	1	14.3
IncDel	1	25.0	IncDel	5	50.0	IncDel	1	100
Decree laws	34	94.4	Decree laws	77	96.3	Decree laws	33	94.3
Total:	45	64.3	Total:	124	68.5	Total:	38	65.5

Figure 2: Rate of Success of Government Bills after the First 13 Months, by 'Programmatic Nature'

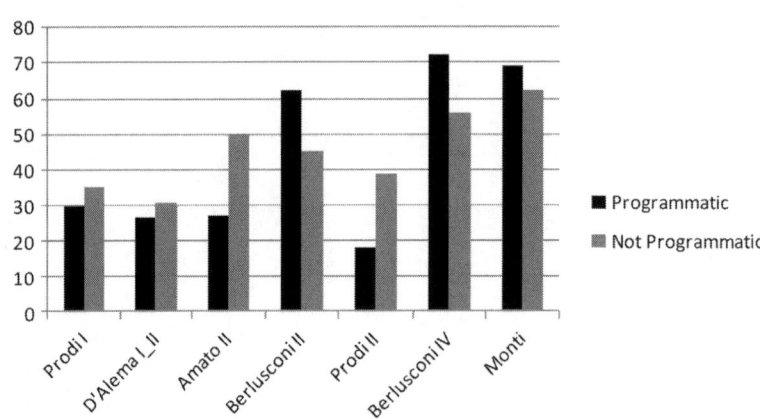

almost all of its crucial decisions through the passing of emergency decrees (Musella, 2012).

We can provide a comparative picture of the success of governmental bills in order to highlight the considerable success of the technical government's measures compared with that of the 'political government' of recent years (Marangoni, 2013). This seems to indicate that the political constraints upon Monti's mandate have worked only partially, by encouraging parliamentary and partisan actors to propose amendments and delays instead of directly opposing the specific proposals made by the government. The overall rate of success of Monti's government bills is impressive (Figure 2), confirming its remarkable record in selecting policy goals. The decision to submit so many emergency decrees guaranteed government an immediate, albeit not automatic, reaction from the parliamentary floor. This would seem to endorse the idea of the government's considerable freedom to fix its own agenda. However, it seems clear that such autonomy was the result of a 'trial and error' approach based on the inclusion of a number of existing proposals, to be discussed with the major parties as of the submission of each single item to parliament.

The Role of Parliamentary Parties

The data analysed in the previous section enabled us to argue that the prime minister and his cabinet of technocrats proved strong enough to impose a selective agenda on parliament. At the same time, this was basically an 'adaptive agenda' characterised by a degree of uncertainty regarding actual outcomes, as well as a lot of bargaining on each single legislative item, in order to see the original policy innovation through to a final vote.

Hence, the question arises as to what the reactions of parliamentary actors were to such proposals. The first thing we are going to look at is the cohesion of parliamentary groups in voting on government bills. In particular, we are going to measure the voting cohesion of the main majority groups during the final stage of voting on each governmental bill in the lower chamber. In order to evaluate groups' voting cohesion, we use the Hix, Noury, and Roland (2007) agreement index (AI). This index measures the extent to which MPs belonging to a given cohort of parliamentarians vote cohesively (that is, in the same way), with abstention as well as 'ayes' and 'nays' considered among the voting options available. For any given parliamentary group, at any given vote, the AI takes a value of one when all MPs (belonging to the group) vote in the same way, and a value of zero when the votes of MPs are equally distributed among the three voting options. In keeping with our main argument, we would expect the centrist and the centre-left components of the government majority to display greater voting cohesiveness (higher AI values) when voting on government bills than the centre-right PDL. Table 4, which shows the average AI values for the main majority groups, confirms our general expectation. The overall values (fourth column) show how both the PD and the new 'centrist pole' (the UDC and the newly founded FLI), at least in general, acted in an extremely cohesive manner in supporting governmental bills (with AI average values of more than 0.98). PDL MPs, on the other hand, have more frequently chosen differing voting options (that is, their support for government bills has been far from unwavering). The table further endorses our argument by disaggregating AI values according to the programmatic nature of the government bills in question (columns 2 and 3). Unlike the other majority groups, in fact, the PDL has been even less compact when voting on the bills linked to the government's programmatic platform (therefore, largely speaking, to Italy's European commitments). These difference are indeed more evident if we use a variant of the AI (AIW) proposed by Giuliani (2008), which weights the original index by the MPs' rate of attendance: for equal values of AI, therefore, the AIW score (in parentheses) decreases as the number of MPs not taking part in the vote increases.[7] The PDL was seen to be split to an even greater degree (overall AIW = 0.60) over their support or otherwise for the governmental bills, with a number of the party's MPs clearly choosing often not to vote in favour of governmental bills

Table 4: Average Values of the Agreement Index of Parliamentary Parties on Government's Bills (Weighted Values in Parentheses)

	Programmatic Bills	Non-programmatic Bills	Overall
PD	0.99 (0.88)	0.98 (0.85)	0.99 (0.86)
UDC	0.99 (0.80)	0.98 (0.82)	0.99 (0.81)
FL	0.99 (0.70)	0.98 (0.69)	0.98 (0.70)
PDL	0.86 (0.57)	0.92 (0.61)	0.89 (0.60)
(N)	(18)	(18)	(36)

Further evidence of the difference in behaviour of the parliamentary groups supporting the cabinet emerges if we examine their reactions to the use of the motion of confidence (*questione di fiducia*) often made by the government to secure the passing of some of its bills, to achieve a rapid decision and to avoid various forms of obstructionism (Marangoni, 2013). Figure 3 indicates the AIW score of the four largest groups (the three groups from the majority, plus the Northern League) for any vote of confidence in the Chamber of Deputies (ordering individual confidence votes according to their respective dates). These data hint at the resistance of partisan actors to the 'imposition' of a series of decisions made by the government. Of course, such resistance may be due to individual rebellion, or to a more systematic strategy employed by a party (or by a party faction) during the parliamentary phase of the legislative process.

The figure shows what could be the strategic behaviour of the PDL compared with the more or less stable support for the government provided by the other parliamentary groups. The overall trend of the PDL's support shows that such support clearly declined over time, which would seem to point to a progressive strategy of 'disengagement' of Berlusconi's party from the government's policy commitments (Giannetti, 2013). Second, a closer examination of these data suggests a clear correlation between the declining support of the centre-right party and the 'macroeconomic' nature of certain measures. While the first dramatic decrease in support (February 2012) was in fact linked to a measure in the field of justice (with the centre-right party criticising Monti and demanding more 'law and order'), all the other cases of critical support from the PDL concerned 'euro-related' measures such as the taxation bill (November 2012) and the

Figure 3: Agreement Index of Parliamentary Parties on Votes of Confidence in the Government in the Chamber of Deputies

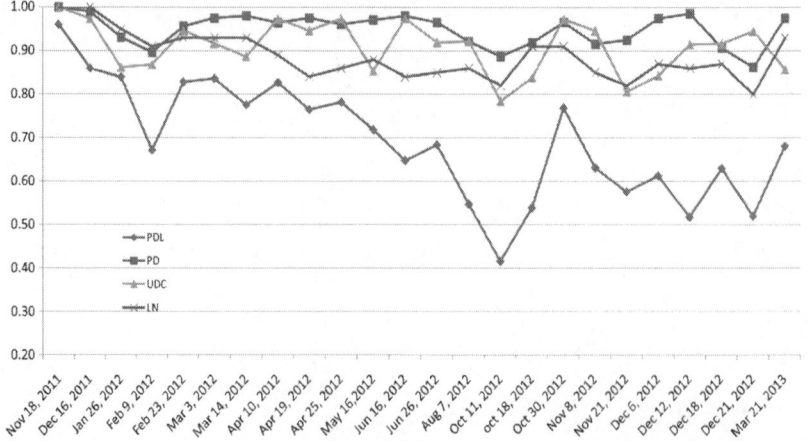

stability pact, containing all the macroeconomic adjustments for the subsequent financial year.

The stance taken by the LN clearly points to agreement within the group (in this case, agreement to oppose the government's proposals). In fact, the limited cases of non-alignment are in fact due to occasional absences, whereas the 58 NL deputies present in parliament displayed 'perfect' discipline notwithstanding the fact that this series of governmental bills was voted on during the most difficult and divisive period in the party's history.[8] Even during this difficult period, the League offered the only genuine opposition to the technocratic government, an opposition grounded in a growing anti-European bias, extremely popular with this party's supporters, and on its rejection of the 'responsibility model', still shared by all the other major political actors.

Conclusion: Towards an Italian-style Grand Coalition?

The evidence presented so far is probably not sufficient to clarify the overall effects of the economic situation on Italy's complex parliamentary democracy. However, the picture we now have of some form of party abdication model may be applied to the period immediately after the advent of the global economic crisis, and in particular during the phase of *mandatory reforms* that Monti's technical government was mandated to introduce.

On the one hand, events point to a clear trend characterised by the superseding of the adversarial model, and the acceptance of an increasingly 'presidentialised' style of policymaking not on the legitimacy of the electoral winner but on the skills of an authoritative technocrat. This phenomenon goes beyond the mere suspension of the rules of party government formation, and applies to the everyday life of government thanks to the personalised style of policymaking adopted by the technocratic premier during his 13 months in office.

On the other hand, a mix of individual and collective behaviour has emerged within the legislative arena, showing the resilience of the parliamentary system and the different strategies adopted by parliamentary parties in order to reduce the implications of such change. Mario Monti and his ministers had to pay special attention to MPs' voting behaviour after proposing new solutions in the European-related policy fields: the vast numbers of amendments from the parliamentary floor, the relatively high degree of disagreement among individual MPs, and forcing the executive to ask for a number of confidence votes on different items of legislation are clear indicators of tension. Moreover, the progressive detachment of the PDL from governmental policymaking points to a strategic rearrangement of the centre-right camp, which in the end allowed Berlusconi to make a rather impressive 'recovery' during the 2013 electoral campaign.

Overall, the strongest evidence we can offer is that supporting our second proposition: keeping constant any specific problems linked to individual opportunism, which in any case did not stop Monti's legislative actions, what clearly emerges from our analysis is the stronger, more durable association between membership of a 'core European' party family and the support (albeit critical and at times subject to negotiation) given to the government's bill. More than ideological or programmatic principles or beliefs, the common denominator in the political discourse of Monti's most loyal supporters – the centrist Catholics and, to a large extent, the centre-left PD – was the need to protect the Europeanist line followed by the premier. In doing so, these actors clearly distanced themselves from their potential partners, who remained isolated within the diminished ranks of the official opposition (the Northern League, a former ally of Berlusconi, and the IdV, a former ally of the PD), while at the same time pointing to the attitude of Berlusconi's followers within the PDL, who officially speaking have always shared a Pro-Europe position (and maintained control over the legislative 'rebels'), but who adopted an increasingly sceptical view of the basic measures proposed by the EU's institutions.

In the end, Monti's inevitable resignation following the PDL's decision to withdraw its support (12 December 2012) has to be ascribed to the same mix of strategic individual behaviour and ideological dissent that emerged within the right wing of the majority. What happened following his resignation confirms the completely transient nature of this political situation: Monti left office clearly expressing his disappointment[9] as a result of the missed opportunity to complete his legislative programme. He remained in charge following the dissolution of parliament, and after considerable thought he decided to enter politics as the leader of a centre coalition (renamed *Scelta Civica* – Civic Choice) during the following electoral campaign. Monti believed he had the chance of a decent electoral pay-off, perhaps enough to be able to form a coalition with the centre-left alliance led by Pierluigi Bersani – leader of the PD and winner of the party's primaries. As we all know, the result of the February general election was a stalemate: the centre-left – the winning coalition by a mere handful of votes – achieved a majority bonus in the lower chamber, but could not form a new government alone (or even with the alliance headed by Monti) because the result in the upper house, the Senate, was a sort of tie, with three blocs (the centre-left, the centre-right led again by Berlusconi, and the new Five Stars Movement led by Beppe Grillo) sharing a similar proportion of seats.

Mutual vetoes prevented the formation of a new government until the sensational re-election of Giorgio Napolitano as president of the Republic was followed by the emergence of a new broad coalition including the PD, PDL, and *Scelta Civica*, which gave its vote of confidence to a government formed by Enrico Letta (28 April 2013). Thus, a new large-scale coalition, albeit less extensive than the one supporting Monti the year before,[10] has continued in the difficult task of dealing with the economic crisis through the constant mediation of opposing policy positions and the substantial employment of technocratic expertise.[11] In a sense, the type of mandate given to this government is very different from the purely technocratic mandate offered to Monti, although there is a clear degree of continuity between the two cases in terms of the reduction in parliamentary relations: whereas Monti was called upon to deal with the crisis during the phase of 'mandatory action', Letta governs during a phase of 'daily bargaining', with constant reference to the key issues raised by the main parties.

It is difficult to say what the real prospects for this sort of Italian-style grand coalition are. It is even more difficult to be sure whether the new competitive system to follow will be based to a greater or lesser degree on a consensual mode of majority–opposition relations. For the purposes of this contribution, we can only point out the importance of the factors we have indicated as strong explanatory variables accounting for the recent deviation from an adversarial mode: in particular, the extremely fragile status of the main parties and their leadership favoured the pronounced form of party abdication witnessed with the technocratic cabinet. Second, the legislative behaviour of those MPs attached to truly 'core European' political groupings proved to be more in keeping with the theme of responsibility, whereas MPs from the other parties displayed a variety of different behaviours, ranging from simple free-riding to a more complex strategic game of negotiations with, and 'rewards' for, government.

Acknowledgements

Luca Verzichelli is responsible for the second and third sections, Francesco Marangoni for the fourth to sixth sections, while the introduction and conclusion were written jointly by the two authors.

Notes

1. The only exception was the party list of *Italia dei Valori*, which was allied to the PD list.
2. As already mentioned, the decision was actually accepted by the rightist *Alleanza Nazionale*, but not by the moderate Catholic party (UDC) led by Pier Ferdinando Casini.
3. The cartel included the PDL and the LN, thus confirming the strategic alliance between Berlusconi and Bossi's movement.
4. It is worth remembering that the technocratic government led by Mr Monti was of a different nature from the government led by Mr. Papademos in Greece (November 2011–May 2012). The latter had a very limited platform (the adoption of the special retrenchment plan imposed by the European *troika*) and a short time frame. The Monti cabinet planned a wide range of economic and budgetary measures, and had the additional goal of lasting to the end of the XVI legislature, thus stimulating parliament to make other important decisions, including that of electoral reform.
5. Bills concerning the ratification of international agreements are excluded, as they have a very limited impact on policy.

6. This was mentioned by Mario Monti himself just after his resignation (at a press conference of 23 December 2012). Answering a question about the failure to reform the electoral system, he reminded listeners of the 'pact' concerning the division of labour between parliament and government: the government was given the task of dealing with the economy and other issues directly dealing with the effects of the crisis, while parliament and its political party groupings were to concern themselves with politics as such.

7. In this way we wish to consider 'not voting' as a possible fourth option, one that MPs may use to indicate their disagreement with (or maybe their indifference towards) a specific bill.

8. The scandal involving the founder and leader of the party, Umberto Bossi, exploded in March 2012. Bossi resigned as federal secretary on 5 April, opening a harsh conflict between his loyalists and the supporter of the future secretary, Roberto Maroni.

9. During the previously mentioned press conference, Monti emphasised the parliamentary obstructionism to a good number of bills, and criticised the lack of any sense of responsibility shown by Silvio Berlusconi.

10. The Letta government was supported by roughly 70 per cent of both senators and deputies, since the Five Star Movement's MPs, the radical left and a few centre-right MPs voted against, while the Northern League abstained.

11. Although the Letta cabinet is composed mainly of politicians, a good number of technocrats and party 'policy experts' are also present. Moreover, the drafting of a new far-reaching constitutional reform has been delegated to a large (42-member) committee of experts appointed mainly from the academic ranks.

References

Chiaramonte, A. (2010). Dal bipolarismo frammentato al bipolarismo limitato? Evoluzione del sistema partitico italiano. In A. Chiaramonte & R. D'Alimonte (Eds.), *Proporzionale se vi pare* (pp. 203–230). Bologna: il Mulino.

Conti, N. (2009). *L'Europa vista dai partiti. Paesi dell'Ue e Italia a confronto*. Pisa: Plus.

Conti, N., & Memoli, V. (2014). Italy. In N. Conti (Ed.), *Party attitudes towards the EU in the member states. Parties for Europe, parties against Europe* (pp. 79–98). London: Routledge.

Fabbrini, S. (2013). Political and institutional constraints on structural reforms: Interpreting the Italian experience. *Modern Italy, 18*(4), 423–436.

Fusaro, C. (2012). La formazione del governo Monti e il ruolo del presidente della Repubblica. In A. Bosco, & D. Mc Donnel (Eds.), *Politica in Italia* (pp. 83–100). Bologna: Il Mulino.

Giannetti, D. (2013). *Il governo tecnico di Mario Monti*. In A. Di Virgilio & C. Radaelli (Eds.), *Politica in Italia* (pp. 141–160). Bologna: Il Mulino.

Giuliani, M. (2008). Patterns of consensual law-making in the Italian parliament. *South European Society & Politics, 13*(1), 61–85.

Hix, S., Noury, A. G., & Roland, G. (2007). *Democratic politics in the European Parliament*. Cambridge: Cambridge University Press.

Mair, P. (2011). *Bini Smaghi vs. the parties: Representative governments and institutional constraints* (EUI Working Papers, RSCAS No. 22).

Marangoni, F. (2012). Technocrats in government: The composition and legislative initiatives of the Monti government eight months into its term of office. *Bulletin of Italian Politics, 3*(1), 135–149.

Marangoni, F. (2013). From fragile majoritarianism to the 'technocratic addendum': Some data on the legislative activity of the governments of the sixteenth legislature. *Contemporary Italian Politics, 5*(1), 71–81.

Moury, C. (2012). *Coalition government and party mandate, how coalition agreements constrain ministerial action*. London: Routledge.

Moury, C., & Timmermans, A. (2008). Conflitto e accordo in governi di coalizione: Il caso Italia. *Rivista Italiana di Scienza Politica, 38*(3), 417–442.

Musella, F. (2012). *Il premier diviso: Italia tra presidenzialismo e parlamentarismo*. Milano: Egea.

Pasquino, G., & Valbruzzi, M. (2012). Non-partisan governments Italian-style: Decision-making and accountability. *Journal of Modern Italian Studies, 17*(5), 612–628.

Roux, C., & Verzichelli, L. (2010). Italy: Still a pro-European, but not a fully Europeanised elite? *South European Society and Politics, 15*(1), 11–33.

Royed, T. (1996). Testing the mandate model in Britain and the United States: Evidence from the Reagan and Thatcher eras. *British Journal of Political Science, 26*(1), 45–80.

Vannucci, A. (2009). The controversial legacy of 'Mani Pulite': A critical analysis of Italian corruption and anti-corruption policies. *Bulletin of Italian Politics, 1*(2), 233–264.

Verzichelli, L., & Cotta, M. (2013, March). *Technical governments, Technicians and non-partisan policy makers in Italy.* Paper presented at the workshop Non-partisan Ministers in European Democracies, Lisbon.

Incumbents, Opposition and International Lenders: Governing Portugal in Times of Crisis

ELISABETTA DE GIORGI, CATHERINE MOURY
and JOÃO PEDRO RUIVO

The Portuguese case provides a unique opportunity to study the opposition's behaviour in a variety of political conditions. It offers an insight into the impact of the financial crisis on the opposition's behaviour in both majority and minority political settings. It allows the comparison of the opposition's relationship with a minority government, during which non-collaboration could have dramatic consequences, and also with a majority govern-ment, when such a choice does not have major political or policy implications. Moreover, it enables us to study the effect of an additional veto player (the so-called troika composed of the European Commission, the European Central Bank and the International Monetary Fund), which not only constrains both majority and opposition parties, but also gives pol-itical entrepreneurs a unique opportunity to push ahead with liberal measures – in this case, clearly in disagreement with the moderate and radical left programmes. Relying on quantitative data on the legislative behaviour of the parliamentary party groups in the period 1995–2012, and on qualitative process-tracking of the opposition's positions on key economic issues – such as the decision to vote against Prime Minister Sócrates' last austerity package after a series of approvals – this article aims to determine whether, and if yes how, the financial crisis has affected the behaviour of the Portuguese opposition parties in parliament, by examining and comparing their behaviour in hard and in normal times.

Introduction

Following the banking collapse in the US and shortly after the beginning of the Greek sovereign debt crisis in the first quarter of 2010, Portugal was pinpointed as a high-risk investment: demands for bonds issued by government shrank and the interest rate shot up. The Prime Minister (PM) José Sócrates kept insisting that the country would not have to be bailed out on the grounds that the minority Socialist government was successfully approving austerity packages with the help of the main opposition party – the Social Democratic Party (PSD). However, in March 2011 the government proposed an additional fourth package that was rejected by all the opposition parties. This led to Sócrates' res-ignation and, shortly after, the international lenders were called in. In the election of June 2011, a centre-right coalition composed of the PSD and the CDS-PP[1] obtained an absolute majority and started to implement a series of painful austerity measures, most of which were conditioned by the international lenders, leading to recession and social unrest. Despite the very liberal and, for many, unfair repercussions of these measures, the Socialist Party (PS) in opposition voted in favour or abstained from voting on the most important packages during the first 15 months of the current legislature, finally shifting strategy and voting against the 2013 budget in November 2012.

This sequence of events implies several puzzles for researchers of Portuguese politics. Why have first the PSD and then the PS supported unpopular and liberal measures for so long? What made them shift from support to opposition? More broadly, what impact has the crisis had on the Portuguese opposition's behaviour? Is there any difference among the opposition parties? How is their behaviour affected by the presence of a majority or minority government?

The Portuguese case provides a unique opportunity to address these questions. It offers an insight into the impact of the financial crisis on the opposition's behaviour with both a minority government, during which non-collaboration could have dramatic consequences, and a majority one, when such a choice rarely has major political or policy implications. It also enables us to study the effect of additional external actors – that is, the European Commission (EC) and later the European Central Bank (ECB) and the International Monetary Fund (IMF) – on the opposition's conduct. These actors not only constrain the majority and opposition, but also represent a precious ally of political entrepreneurs who would like to push ahead with liberal measures – in this case, clearly in disagreement with both the moderate and radical left parties' programmes.

Our main argument is that economic crises, which jeopardise national interest but also trigger extremely radical socio-economic measures, have an important effect on the opposition's behaviour. We observe that consensus in parliament decreased with the onset of the current crisis mainly because more salient and divisive socio-economic policies had to be approved. However, we also expect and observe variations among parties; on the one hand the mainstream opposition parties are more consensual than they would be if the same policies were presented in normal times (as long as they do not see a golden opportunity to get into power themselves), and on the other hand, the radical parties are even more adversarial than usual. In order to demonstrate these claims, we rely on qualitative process-tracking of the Portuguese opposition's positions on key economic issues (including interviews with key political players) and on quantitative data on the voting behaviour of the parliamentary party groups before and after the crisis (in the period 1995–2012).

Theoretical Argument and Hypotheses

As specified in the introduction, opposition parties are always exposed to two contrasting pressures: one towards conflict, which comes from the need to mark their position as different from that of the government in office, and one towards cooperation, which comes from the will to take part in decision-making and influence the policy outcome. With the financial crisis, this dilemma between conflict and cooperation has become even more crucial. Austerity measures are unpopular and, in bad economic times, voters are more likely to withdraw their support for the government in office (Lewis-Beck, 1988). Thus, the opposition parties have a choice between the need to cooperate with the majority for the nation's sake and the opportunity to weaken a fragile government even further and possibly get into power at the subsequent election.

Little is said in the existing literature about the possible behaviour of the opposition parties in such a critical situation. Previous research suggests that the opposition's behaviour is likely to be more adversarial on economic and social policies (De Giorgi, 2011; Rose, 1984) and on more salient issues (Carammia & De Giorgi, 2011; Mújica & Sánchez-Cuenca, 2006; Stecker, 2011). As the legislation presented by the governments to tackle the crisis is mainly related to socio-economic issues and innately salient policies, our first hypothesis is:

> *H1: Since the beginning of the crisis, the level of consensus between the government and opposition parties in Portugal has decreased as the number of socio-economic and salient policies discussed in parliament has increased.*

However, the nature of parties and the type of party competition constitute another crucial variable affecting the behaviour of the opposition in parliament (Duverger, 1954; Flanagan, 2001; Sartori, 1966). In particular, the mainstream (and more moderate) parties that alternate in government are more inclined to act responsibly than the more radical ones, which are usually permanently in opposition (Sartori, 1966, p. 35).

This difference between permanent and alternative opposition has implications for our research question, namely the impact of the crisis on the opposition behaviour: because the legislation presented by the governments to save their country from the economic crisis is of the highest national interest, we expect mainstream parties to feel 'responsible' and cooperate with the government even though they would have opposed these policies under normal circumstances. On the other hand, radical opposition parties are expected to take advantage of the crisis and emphasise their dissimilarity with the government even further. Thus, although we expect a general decrease in the level of consensus after the onset of the crisis in Portugal (due to the rising number of salient and socio-economic policy decisions), we expect the net impact of the crisis on the opposition behaviour to vary from one party to another. Since the onset of the crisis, the mainstream parties that usually alternate in government in Portugal, namely the PS, the PSD and the CDS-PP, have been expected to behave more consensually than in normal times. We expect the contrary to be true for the radical left parties (the PCP, PEV and BE).[2] Therefore, our second hypothesis states that:

H2: Controlling for saliency and type of policies, since the onset of the crisis the mainstream opposition parties have been more consensual than the radical parties.

In this turbulent period, there is one further intervening variable that cannot be ignored, namely the increasing influence of international actors on the economic policy issue. Indeed, the bailout meant that the conditions set by the EC, the ECB and the IMF forced the Portuguese government to make radical changes in their policies. However, even before the bailout the EC had pressed for public debt and deficit to be reduced as quickly as possible. According to previous research, Euroscepticism – and conversely pro-Europeanism – has a significant impact on the government–opposition dynamics and party competition (Hooghe, Marks, & Wilson, 2004; Sitter, 2001, 2002; Szczerbiak & Taggart, 2003). We expect the traditionally pro-European parties in opposition to be more likely to cooperate with the government when the socio-economic measures follow the EU recommendations/orders (with or without the intervention of the IMF). Alternatively, we expect the more Eurosceptic parties in opposition to have fewer incentives to collaborate when the EU is influencing legislation.

H3: Pro-European parties in opposition are more likely to cooperate with the government on policies recommended by the European Union than Eurosceptic parties.

Obviously, this third hypothesis is related to the former as parties that are permanently out of government tend to be more Eurosceptic (Sitter, 2001; Taggart, 1998), while Eurosceptic parties that want to become credible coalition partners frequently moderate their hostility to Europe (Conti & De Giorgi, 2011; Costa Lobo & Magalhães, 2011). Two different kinds of analysis – one based on interviews with Portuguese MPs conducted at the beginning of the crisis in 2008 (Moury & De Sousa, 2011), and the other based on the study of party manifestos in the period from 1995 to 2005 (Costa Lobo & Magalhães, 2011) – indeed converge to show that the two major parties, the PS and PSD, have a very strong pro-European attitude. However, these studies also show a difference within both mainstream and opposition parties. While the manifestos of the three radical left parties (Leftist Bloc BE, the Communist PCP and the Greens PEV), which have never been in government, present strong anti-European stances, Moury and De Sousa (2011) observed that a large majority of BE deputies believes that EU membership is a good thing (66·7 per cent), in contrast to the small minority (29 per cent) of the CDU (PCP-PEV) deputies who agree with this statement. Similarly, the CDS-PP is less pro-Europe than its centre-right partner; this difference can be observed both in the manifestos and in interviews, with a lower proportion of deputies from CDS-PP welcoming EU membership than of PSD deputies (87 per cent versus 97 per cent). Thus, if *H3* is correct, after the crisis we should observe a variation in the voting behaviour between the CDS-PP and the two other mainstream parties on the one hand and between the BE and the CDU on the other.

Our final hypothesis is related to the variation in time during the period of crisis. As stated above, austerity measures are unpopular and so it is the government that is constrained to implement them. As a consequence, the main opposition parties have a better chance during the financial crisis of replacing the incumbents if new elections occur. So the more the government is in jeopardy (because it is a minority government or because there is intra-coalitional dissension) and the better the prospect of the opposition parties winning office in the case of election, the greater the opposition's incentives to challenge – rather than to support – the executive.[3] Hence, our last research hypothesis is the following:

> H4: After the onset of the crisis, the opposition parties will be more adversarial when their possibilities to replace the government in office increase.

In the next two sections, we test these four hypotheses, first in light of process-tracking of the main events and bills approved in parliament since the start of the crisis, and second through a quantitative data analysis of the legislation passed before and after the crisis, in the period from 1995 to 2012.

A Political Overview of the Crisis

Opposition's Behaviour and Narratives (2008–12)

After the fall of Lehman Brothers in September 2008, there was a dramatic slowdown in the Portuguese economy. As exchange devaluation was not an option – unlike in the previous debt crises in the 1970s and 1980s – the initial measure taken by the first Sócrates government (a single-party majority government) was fiscal expansion. These counter-cyclical fiscal policies were taken in coordination with the EU's initial neo-Keynesian approach to the crisis (European Commission, 2008). These proposals received different responses in parliament, with all opposition parties voting against the 2009 budget, but in favour of its first amendment (with the exception of the PSD, which voted against). Nonetheless, the reasons behind the negative votes of the various parties were very different: while the radical left parties criticised the PS for not going far enough, the PSD and CDS-PP considered the expansionary budget to be irresponsible.

During the second half of 2009, the Portuguese government had reported an estimated 2·6 per cent slump in gross domestic product and a public deficit of 9·3 per cent in 2009. The European Council urged the country to engage rapidly in policies aimed at medium-term fiscal consolidation (European Council, 2009), thus putting an end to the short cycle of fiscal expansion. In April 2010, the Greek government asked for financial assistance from the EU to avoid bankruptcy, while the Portuguese government's interest rates soared to their highest level since entry into the eurozone. As the incumbent PS had lost the absolute majority in parliament when a general election was called in September 2009, the new Socialist minority government urged the parliamentary opposition to help approve the budget for 2010. According to Portuguese economists, this budget was not a real austerity plan. Nevertheless, the freezing of public sector salaries and the plan to reduce state personnel carried the message that needed to be heard by the markets and the EU leaders. The left-wing parties accused international financial speculators of robbing the country with the acquiescence of the government and rejected the bill. While blaming the previous Socialist governments (of both Guterres and Sócrates) for getting the country into trouble, the PSD and the CDS abstained from voting and let the budget pass.

Just three days after the budget's approval, on 12 March, the government went back to parliament to ask for support for the Stability and Growth Programme (SGP) 2010–13, before delivering it to the EU. Unlike the budget, the SGP was undoubtedly an austerity package composed of a wide set of hard fiscal measures. Both the CDS and the radical left parties soon announced they would vote against it. For the parliamentary left, the Portuguese governments had mistakenly followed the path of recessionary budget policies that would not only fail to solve the debt crisis but also destroy the national economy, dismantle the welfare state and increase social inequalities. The CDS, for its part, blamed the Socialist government for targeting the poor and most vulnerable and lacking a strategy to lead the country back to growth. Despite sharing a similar discourse, the PSD (just before the election of its new leader Pedro Passos Coelho) decided to negotiate the first austerity package and abstained from voting: political stability was of greater national interest, especially after Fitch's downgrading of the Portuguese credit rating.

By the end of the first quarter of 2010, Portugal was boarding the Greek ship and starting to muddle through the storm of recessionary austerity packages, reports of negative growth, rising unemployment and poor fiscal behaviour, downgrading credit rates, and spiking yields. Despite an ever critical stance towards the government, the PSD negotiated two additional austerity packages with the PS and abstained from voting on them once in parliament. Whenever talks with the government broke down, the president of the Republic (PR), Aníbal Cavaco Silva, pushed the PSD – the party he had led in the 1980s and 1990s – back to the negotiating table.

Such a cycle would eventually come to an end in early 2011, when the government lost support from all sides of the political spectrum, in particular from the PR. While the three initial packages of the Sócrates government had been sustained by the president, Cavaco Silva's re-election in January 2011 marked a turning point. In February, the president vetoed a decree law for the first time in five years of cohabitation with the PS in government. His inauguration speech soon afterwards, on 9 March 2011, was regarded by many politicians and observers as a 'declaration of war' to the government. The scene was set for an institutional conflict between the PR and the government.

In the meantime, the government was forced to negotiate a fourth austerity package with the EU, which basically consisted of an amended version of the SGP (Stability and Growth Pact) 2011–14. According to the PSD, the negotiations were conducted behind the backs of the parliamentary opposition and the PR. Although there was no formal need to approve this new version of the SGP in parliament, the PM declared he would resign if the opposition proposed a resolution against the programme which received a majority vote in parliament. Rejecting the government package would therefore trigger a political crisis in the middle of a financial storm, and the opposition should be blamed accordingly. This behaviour made many observers conclude that the PM was keen to make the government fail before the bailout by also blaming the opposition parties for their lack of responsibility.

Despite the pressure of new rating downgrades, the PR did not take action to rescue the plan from rejection on the grounds that the presidency had been prevented from using its influence owing to the lack of information given by the government on the new austerity package. The PSD voted against it and the PM immediately resigned. The main arguments used by the PSD to explain its shift in voting behaviour and the rejection of the fourth and last austerity package of the PS executive were the eroded authority and credibility of the socialists in managing the crisis, as well as the alleged negotiations of the fourth austerity package with the European authorities behind the backs of parliament, the president and the social partners. In the aftermath of these events, the caretaker government had no choice but to ask for the bailout on 6 April, at the beginning of the electoral campaign.

The negotiating process was conducted by the government on behalf of the Portuguese Republic and a memorandum of understanding was signed in May by the lenders – the so-called *troika*, composed of the EC, the ECB and the IMF – and the three mainstream parties: the PS, PSD and CDS. This was a signal that, no matter which party was going to win the election, the new government would inevitably be constrained by the commitments to its international lenders. By contrast, the radical parties (PCP, PEV and BE) claimed that the bailout was undemocratic and unnecessary and refused to participate in discussions with the *troika*.

At the general election held in June 2011, the centre-right coalition (PSD and CDS-PP) obtained an absolute majority and the head of the PSD, Pedro Passos Coelho, became the new PM. As the agent of the *troika*, Coelho's government had to implement a series of painful austerity measures, triggering recession and social unrest. Once in opposition, the PS started to blame the government for the ever worsening crisis, thus aligning its discourse with the more radical parties on the left. Despite this common discourse and the actual 'irrelevance' of its voting choice in the current majority setting, the PS had been quite cooperative on the major policy packages proposed by the government until November 2012 (and arguably more painful and inconsistent with its ideological background). While the three radical left parties constantly voted against the government packages, the PS abstained from voting on both the 2012 budget, which included tax increases and public sector wage cuts, and the new labour legislation, which introduced cuts in pay and holidays and the easing of restrictions on lay-offs and workers' dismissals. In addition, the socialists voted in favour of amending the legal regimes on the recapitalisation and consolidation of the banking sector with the help of the state and the privatisations of state-owned enterprises. Finally, the PS also approved the ratification of the EU Fiscal Compact in April 2012 (with Portugal being the first member state to ratify the treaty). The need to act responsibly vis-à-vis the 2011 bailout agreement that all were prepared to sign was again the main reason behind their choices (according to the socialist deputies interviewed).[4] However, a shift was observed in November 2012 when the PS voted against both a second amendment to the 2012 budget and the 2013 budget – blaming the government for its incompetence and stubborn insistence on austerity, and failure to take action to foster economic growth. From then on, the socialists tended to align their legislative behaviour with the parties on the left, voting against some critical and highly politicised bills, all framed by the crisis: the merging of local government constituencies, the regulation of labour relations in the private sector (cuts in compensations for dismissals) and in the public sector (reducing the security of the work contract, and increasing the weekly working hours), and a new austerity budget for 2014. In addition, the PS also started to request a review of the constitutionality of austerity laws approved by the centre-right majority. In key issues the Court has ruled in favour of the socialists, thus pushing the government to find alternative measures under the oversight and pressure of the *troika*. On some occasions, though, the PS kept a distance from the leftist opposition parties, especially when the recapitalisation of the banking sector or fostering private investments (through tax credits) was at stake.

Understanding the Opposition's Choices

As stated already, the above narratives offer several puzzles. What can explain first the PSD and then the PS support of unpopular government measures? What can justify a shift in the conduct of those parties at one given moment in time? And what reasons can be found for the variation among parties?

The answer to the first question lies in the risk involved in the crisis, namely default and bankruptcy – a matter of great national interest – for which the two major parties, the PS and the PSD, felt responsible even from the opposition benches (*H2*). Although it is true that the socialists and the centre-right parties had been ideologically close for decades,[5] few of the bills just mentioned would have got the support of the major opposition parties in normal times. It seems that the PSD and PS had felt constrained by a sense of responsibility and, for the latter, by the commitment to fulfil the agreement signed with the international lenders.

This sense of obligation was not shared by the radical left parties or the CDS-PP. As has been said, the permanent exclusion of the former from government might help to explain their adversarial conduct even in hard times (*H2*), but this does not help us to understand the CDS-PP's controversial behaviour. Here the pro- or anti-European attitudes could contribute to our investigation (*H3*). As noted above, the PS and PSD are as unequivocally pro-European as the CDU is Eurosceptic; however, the CDS-PP and the BE are more ambiguous about Europe. This ambiguity might help explain why the CDS-PP was less inclined to consensus than its social democratic ally, despite its ambition to govern. Similarly, the pro-European stance of the PS and PSD (together with their centrality in the political spectrum) might contribute to explaining their collaboration with the government on relevant socio-economic legislation. On the other hand, the Euroscepticism of the radical left parties sheds additional light on why they have systematically opposed the government's measures in times of crisis.

One last puzzle tabled by the Portuguese story has to do with the reason why, after three crucial abstentions, the PSD finally decided to vote for a resolution against the fourth austerity package proposed by the Socialist government and why a similar shift was observed in the PS behaviour from November 2012. We hypothesise that these decisions were taken because the main opposition parties' possibilities to gain office in the case of an election had increased significantly immediately prior to these specific moments. The intentions of vote in the 2010–12 period (Figure 1) in fact show that both the PSD and the PS changed their voting behaviour from cooperative to conflictual when the electorate's

Figure 1: Evolution of Vote Intention for the PS and PSD (March 2010–January 2013)

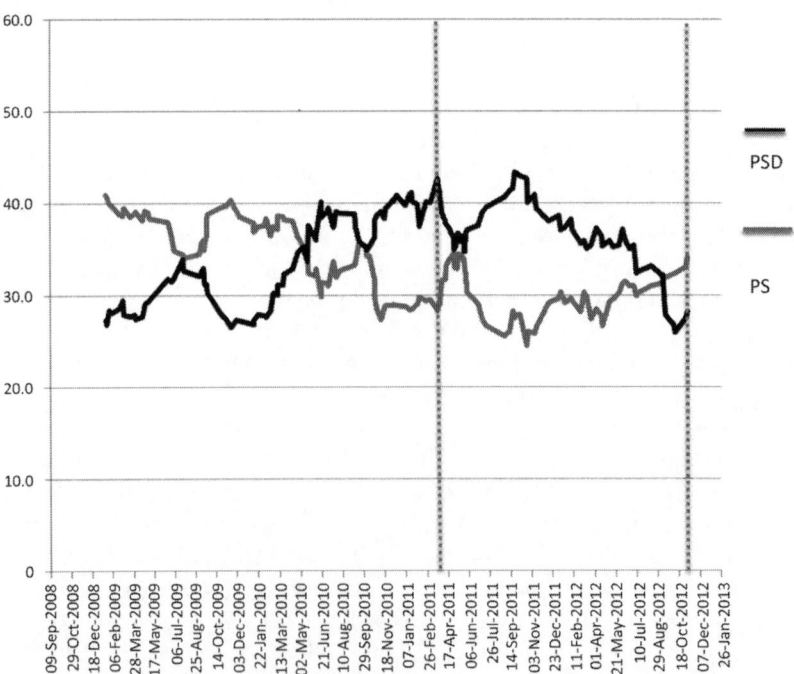

Source: http://margensdeerro.blogspot.pt by Pedro Magalhães.

voting intentions moved in their favour. As shown in Figure 1, the voting intentions were in favour of the PS when the first two packages were voted upon and
were almost even between the PS and PSD when the third one was approved; but
the PSD had a clear edge when the fourth package was presented to parliament.
Supported by voting intention polls and probably under significant internal
pressure from its party and the PR himself (Magalhães, 2012), Passos Coelho
chose to join the rest of the opposition parties in rejecting the additional
package proposed by the PS. This move led to a significant decrease in its
support so that the election results were actually quite vague.

A similar dynamic could be observed for the PS in opposition. After abstaining from voting for the major socio-economic measures proposed by the centre-
right government during the first 15 months of the current legislature, the PS
decided to vote against the government's proposal in November 2012 – a time
when polls on voting intentions gave it an edge over the PSD (and the governing
coalition was showing clear signs of internal conflict).

Therefore, while a sense of responsibility and pro-European attitudes pushed
the two larger parties to cooperate with the government even from the opposition
benches, this support had a limit: when a party could make the government fall
and/or had a good chance of winning if there were an election, self-interest
prevailed.

Interviews with key players at the time of the crisis support this explanation.
As a former PSD minister said when asked about what explained the decision to
vote against the fourth austerity package in March 2011: 'If the opposition sees
that the life expectancy of the government is long, then it will let the measures
pass; if, on the contrary ... the opposition party sees an opportunity to get in
power itself, obviously it will start to oppose the government measures'. A
similar reasoning was made by a former junior minister from the PS: 'In Portugal,
no one accepts that the opposition is against everything at the beginning of its
mandate. There is the feeling that a party that aspires to govern should adopt a
responsible behaviour. But there are also some political strategies at stake:
now [January 2013] the opinion polls give the edge to the PS. As the crisis
always brings governmental instability, the PS knows that it is just a matter of
time before it will be back in government'.

Comparing Opposition in Normal and Hard Times: Quantitative Data Analysis

Although the qualitative data analysed so far tell an interesting story, the focus on
the most important socio-economic measures might create a distorted view of the
overall reality. We therefore decided to rely also on more quantitative data and
analyse the opposition's voting behaviour on the final approval of the laws in parliament from 1995 onwards. We focused on: two Socialist minority governments,
one during Portugal's 'golden years' of economic growth (Guterres I, 1995–99)
and the other in the period just after the onset of the financial crisis (Sócrates II,

2009–11); two majority coalition governments (PSD and CDS-PP), the first in relatively good economic times (Barroso II, 2002–4) and the second just after the bailout (the current Passos Coelho, 2011–); and one single-party majority government, which was in charge before and after the beginning of the crisis (Sócrates I, 2005–9). This broad scope allows us to compare the opposition's voting behaviour in normal and hard times and test the influence of further variables mentioned in our hypotheses.[6]

The Dependent Variable

As we have said, we investigated the voting behaviour of the Portuguese parliamentary parties and chose the consensual voting of the opposition party groups in parliament as our dependent variable. In order to measure the level of *consensus* shown by the Portuguese opposition during the five selected governments, we shall refer to the favourable voting behaviour during the final stage of the law-making process. The information refers to the parliamentary party groups' voting choice on all the approved laws other than those dealing with administrative reorganisation. As the online archive also enables us to identify how many MPs voted against their own group, we were able to employ Capo's index of consensus in parliament, used by Mújica and Sánchez-Cuenca (2006):

$$\text{Consensus in parliament} = \frac{vf}{(n^*v)/N}$$

where vf stands for the number of votes for the law, n for the number of MPs belonging to the main party, v for the total number of cast votes, and N for the size of the Assembly. If the index has value '1', the incumbent party does not obtain support from any other parliamentary group. If the index has a value over '1', the incumbent gets support from other groups: the more the support, the higher the number.

The Operationalisation of the Independent and Controlling Variables

As noted above, our main assumption is that the crisis has had an impact on the level of consensus in parliament. So a dummy variable has been created to identify the beginning of the crisis, even though there is no straightforward definition of when the crisis really started. The fall of Lehman Brothers on 15 September 2008 is considered by many observers as the official 'beginning' of the world crisis. Hence, we built one dummy variable taking the value '1' after 15 September and '0' before. But in order to capture the effect of the Portuguese bailout on the opposition's behaviour, we created another dummy taking value '1' after 6 April 2011 and '0' before. We expect both these variables to be negatively related to the level of consensus in parliament.

In order to test the net effect of the crisis, we decided to control for four variables that are likely to influence opposition voting behaviour. First, the policy area: socio-economic policies are expected to be more conflictual because parties are expected to represent different socio-economic interests. Thus, we classified each law following the 21 categories of the Comparative Agendas Policy Project[7] and then created a dummy variable to distinguish the laws dealing with the socio-economic policy sector – which is the sum of four different policy areas, respectively called macroeconomic issues, general labour and employment, general social welfare, general banking and finance – from all the others. We called this variable *Socio-economic sector* and we expect it to be negatively associated with the opposition's propensity to vote yes or to abstain rather than to vote no.

Second, the type of government: Portugal has experienced alternating types of government – coalition and single-party, majority and minority. The concentration of the executive power in a strong single-party majority cabinet gives the opposition very different political opportunities in parliament, compared with those given by the concentration of the executive in either a minority government or a coalition government. In the first case, the parliamentary opposition has neither space for nor interest in intervening or negotiating with the government in office, which is already supported by a strong and usually disciplined single-party majority. At the same time, this situation obliges the official parliamentary opposition to propose itself as constructive and alternative, in order to compete for power at the following election. In the second case, the life of parliamentary opposition seems to be more advantageous, particularly for smaller parties, which are the government's crucial allies so as to obtain the majority in parliament (essential in the case of minority government, and sometimes necessary when intra-coalition divergence occurs). As the opposition parties might behave differently depending on the type of government in office, we decide to control this variable (*Majority government*).

It is also believed that the author of the bill affects the level of cooperation between majority and opposition (De Giorgi & Marangoni, 2009; Mújica & Sánchez-Cuenca, 2006). This is so because by definition the parliamentary opposition opposes the government (Dahl, 1966). We therefore assume that the opposition will be more adversarial when a government bill is at stake. As a control variable, we thus created a dichotomous variable (*Initiative*), which assumes value '1' when the law in question is proposed by the government or any majority party member and value '0' otherwise.

Finally, some scholars emphasise that the characteristics of the legislative acts are likely to have a substantive effect on the patterns of voting behaviour. Giuseppe Di Palma (1977) showed how the high degree of consensualism found in the lawmaking process in the first four legislatures of the Italian Republic was largely due to the poor quality of the laws enacted. In a widely polarised and fragmented party system, an impressive number of *leggine* (small laws) limited in both scope and policy comprehensiveness helped parliamentary actors to find the necessary compromise and agreement. Speculating a little on these acknowledgements, we expect the opposition to be more consensual on legislation that is limited in policy comprehensiveness (and hence, less relevant). As a result, we use the number of committees involved in the lawmaking process as a proxy for the political relevance of each bill and it is also controlled.

Opposition in Normal and Hard Times: A Description

Do we observe any difference after the crisis in terms of types of law approved and the consequent level of conflict created in parliament? Our first hypothesis is based on the assumption that a larger number of relevant bills dealing with socio-economic issues has been approved since the start of the crisis in Portugal and that both the relevance and the issue area of a given bill have an impact on the opposition's voting behaviour. By examining the content of the laws approved during the five governments under analysis, we can actually observe a clear increase in the amount of legislation dealing with relevant and socio-economic policies in the years of the financial crisis (Table 1).

Whereas socio-economic laws are never more than 24 per cent of the total in the first three governments under analysis, they reach 34·5 per cent of the total legislation during both the second Sócrates government and the current Passos Coelho government. Furthermore, in Table 1 we can see a clear increase in the average number of committees involved in the approval process of these bills. Thus, owing to the rise of both the number of socio-economic bills and their level of comprehensiveness (given by the increasing number of committees involved in their approval), we would expect the level of conflict in parliament to increase as well.

Table 2 presents the average index of consensus per legislature. In the last row we can see that, on average, the Portuguese parliament is quite consensual: the index is well above unity for each legislature and on average more than one-third of the bills are passed with a positive vote from every parliamentary group

Table 1: Average Percentage of Socio-economic Laws, Number of Words and Committees per Legislature

	Percentage of Laws Approved Dealing with Socio-economic Issues	Average Number of Committees Involved
Guterres I (1995–99)	23.7	1.3
Barroso (2002–4)	17.7	1.2
Sócrates I (2005–9)	22.2	1.4
Sócrates II (2009–11)	34.5	2.5
Passos Coelho (2011–)	34.5	2.9

Table 2: Index of Consensus per Legislature and Percentage of Votes for which every Parliamentary Group Votes in Favour, All Legislation (and Important Legislation Only)

Legislature	Capo's Index	Number of Unanimous Laws (%)	N
Guterres I (PS, minority)	1.66 (1.69)	42.6 (44.2)	357 (95)
Barroso (PSD/CDS-PP, majority)	1.55 (1.38)	34.1 (25.8)	167 (31)
Sócrates I (PS, majority)	1.52 (1.54)	30.5 (35.0)	344 (40)
Sócrates II (PS, minority)	1.62 (1.67)	27.3 (42.9)	88 (7)
Passos Coelho (PSD/CDS-PP, majority)	1.31 (1.23)	11.1 (10.5)	54 (19)
Average:	1.61 (1.58)	34.1 (35.9)	1010 (192)

in parliament. But a look at Table 3 also grants some support to our hypothesis concerning the negative impact of the crisis on the voting behaviour of the opposition in parliament: if we compare the two Socialist minority governments led by Guterres and Sócrates or the two PSD/CDS coalition governments led by Barroso and Passos Coelho – thus keeping both the variable type of government and party in office constant – we observe a decrease in the level of consensus after the crisis in both cases (especially if we compare the two centre-right governments). Our first hypothesis seems to be confirmed. As it might be argued that the above numbers mix very important and more trivial legislation, Table 2 also presents the main index of consensus for pieces of legislation that went through at least two committees (one-fifth of the total of all bills) – thus more inclusive and probably more relevant in terms of policy comprehensiveness. If we look at the percentage of laws that are passed unanimously, we observe the same downward trends – which are particularly clear for the centre-right governments.

Table 3 presents some descriptive statistics about the voting behaviour of each opposition party during the five governments under analysis. As we can see, the opposition parties vote together with the government much more often than they abstain or vote against. Crossing the average per party with the average per legislature, we can see that the Portuguese opposition parties voted in favour of legislation almost half of the time, while they abstained 20 per cent and voted against only 30 per cent of the time. The figures are broadly the same when we look at important legislation only (with a slightly higher percentage of positive votes). However, we do observe variation across time and parties. Most importantly, Table 3 shows how the proportion of negative votes is lower during minority governments (Guterres I and Sócrates II) and how radical left parties are significantly less inclined to consensus than mainstream parties (see the last column on the right). These findings hold for both the entire legislation and the subset of relevant legislation only.

Table 3: Percentage of No, Yes and Abstention Votes per Opposition Party and per Government

		Guterres I	Barroso	Sócrates I	Sócrates II	Passos Coelho	Average
PS	No		24 (36)			20	23
						(16)	(28)
	Yes		62			51	59
			(46)			(47)	(46)
	Abst.		14			29	18
			(18)			(37)	(26)
PSD	No	12		22	9.0		17
		(10)		(24)	(0.0)		(15)
	Yes	61		60	64		61
		(64)		(60)	(40)		(61)
	Abst.	27		19	27		23
		(26)		(17)	(60)		(24)
CDS-PP	No	12		25	17		19
		(15)		(26)	(20)		(15)
	Yes	64		49	60		56
		(68)		(50)	(40)		(61)
	Abst.	24		26	27		25
		(17)		(23)	(40)		(24)
CDU*	No	16	39	45	34	59	35
		(16)	(50)	(34)	(60)	(42)	(31)
	Yes	64	47	37	48	14	47
		(60)	(39)	(49)	(40)	(26)	(48)
	Abst.	21	14	18	19	28	19
		(25)	(11)	(17)	(0.0)	(32)	(21)
BE	No		43	32	55	44	44
			(61)	(32)	(60)	(42)	(31)
	Yes		43	53	24	40	40
			(29)	(54)	(40)	(26)	(48)
	Abst.		14	15	22	16	17
			(11)	(15)	(0.0)	(32)	(21)
Total:	No	14	37	34	29	45	31
		(14)	(49)	(29)	(35)	(33)	(24)
	Yes	63	50	47	48	31	48
		(64)	(38)	(53)	(45)	(33)	(53)
	Abst.	23	14	19	22	25	21
		(24)	(13)	(18)	(25)	(33)	(23)

Note: We excluded the bills presented exclusively by the opposition party groups from the analysis. In parentheses important bills only ($N = 1009$ and 116).
*We initially codified the two groups PCP and PEV separately, but we present them together for the sake of clarity, as their voting behaviour is almost identical.

Comparing minority and coalition governments before and after the crisis, Table 3 also indicates that the impact of the crisis on the PS and PSD, which vote less frequently against the government after the crisis (and abstain more often), is very different from the impact on the CDS-PP and on the PCP and PEV, for which the opposite is true. As for the BE, no significant difference is observable across time during the two governments. If we look at the most important legislation only, the difference in time is even more marked for the PS and PSD (in the decrease in 'nays' and the increase in 'abstentions') and for the CDS-PP (in the decrease in 'ayes'). As far as the PCP and PEV are concerned, we see a huge increase in 'nays' from Guterres to Sócrates II, but a decrease from Barroso to Passos Coelho. Finally, the BE clearly voted 'no' on the most important legislation more often before the crisis than after.

The Analysis

In order to isolate the effect of the crisis on opposition voting behaviour from other possible intervening variables, we computed a multinomial logistic regression. In Table 4, we evaluate the impact of a series of variables on each party's propensity to vote yes or abstain rather than to vote no. Together with the controlling variables specified above, we insert – as our main independent variable – a dummy for the start of the crisis (the fall of Lehman Brothers on 15 September 2008) and for the date of the Portuguese bailout (7 April 2011).[8] We observe a significant independent effect of the crisis on the opposition parties' behaviour but, as expected, the direction of the change varies from one party to another according to its governing aspirations and European attitudes.

Table 4 shows that the two most pro-European parties, the PS and the PSD, which have always alternated in government, tend to act more consensually after the beginning of the crisis than they did before, *ceteris paribus*. The PS, for example, is almost twice as likely to abstain – rather than to vote no – since the bailout and international intervention. Similarly, the PSD, which came into power just after the bailout, was actually 50 per cent more likely to abstain rather than to vote no after the fall of Lehman Brothers. By contrast, everything being constant, remarkably the PCP and PEV appear to be less likely to vote yes rather than no after the start of the crisis and the bailout.[9] No independent effect of the crisis could be found for the CDS-PP, whereas for the BE the start of the crisis increased (rather than decreased, as we would expect) the odds of abstaining rather than voting no by 66 per cent.

Three groups of parties can thus be distinguished according to the impact the crisis has had so far on their behaviour: the PS and PSD, which appear to have been, *ceteris paribus*, less adversarial since the crisis began; the PCP and PEV, for which the contrary is true; and the CDS-PP and BE, for which no significant influence could be identified. This corresponds with our expectations in *H2* and *H3*: from the mainstream and very pro-EU PS and PSD, to the radical and Euro-sceptic PCP and PEV, the CDS-PP and the BE being subject to contradictory forces (governmental ambition but ambiguity on the EU for the CDS-PP, and permanency of opposition but moderate Euroscepticism for the BE). These findings thus support *H2* and *H3* that the crisis would have contradictory effects according to whether the parties are permanently in opposition (or not) on the one hand and their pro- or anti-European stances on the other.

Also in line with our expectations, most of the controlling variables proved to have a significant impact on the opposition's voting behaviour in parliament. First, we see that when we have a minority government, all opposition parties

Table 4: Factors Affecting the Decision of Opposition Parties to Vote Yes or to Abstain rather than Vote No (Excluding Votes on Initiatives from the Opposition)

	PS Yes B (Sig.)	PS Abst. B (Sig.)	PSD Yes B (Sig.)	PSD Abst. B (Sig.)	CDS-PP Yes B (Sig.)	CDS-PP Abst. B (Sig.)	PCP Yes B (Sig.)	PCP Abst. B (Sig.)	PEV Yes B (Sig.)	PEV Abst. B (Sig.)	BE Yes B (Sig.)	BE Abst. B (Sig.)
Intercept	0.42 (0.341)	−0.40 (0.437)	0.93** (0.003)	−0.20 (0.586)	0.79** (0.008)	0.01 (0.974)	−0.11 (0.622)	−0.73** (0.006)	−0.13 (0.556)	−0.76** (0.04)	−0.19 (0.473)	−1.26*** (0.001)
Majority government	—	—	0.71*** (0.001)	1.19*** (0.000)	0.95*** (0.000)	0.80*** (0.001)	1.42*** (0.000)	1.09*** (0.000)	1.42*** (0.000)	1.13*** (0.000)	0.38 (0.27)	0.29 (0.503)
Simple bills (less than one committee)	0.60 (0.173)	0.00 (1.000)	−0.03 (0.907)	−0.15 (0.655)	−0.00 (0.993)	0.05 (0.881)	−0.09 (0.682)	−0.17 (0.504)	−0.07 (0.759)	−0.20 (0.434)	0.16 (0.526)	0.20 (0.58)
Socio-economic bill	−2.03*** (0.000)	−0.65 (0.199)	−0.91 (0.000)***	0.03 (0.901)	−0.89*** (0.000)	−0.13 (0.625)	−1.00*** (0.000)	−0.96*** (0.000)	−0.91*** (0.000)	−0.89*** (0.001)	−0.93*** (0.000)	−1.52*** (0.000)
Multiparty bills	1.16* (0.016)	0.18 (0.774)	0.90*** (0.000)	−0.40 (0.198)	0.58** (0.010)	−0.69* (0.016)	1.34*** (0.000)	0.30 (0.208)	1.39*** (0.000)	0.39 (0.107)	1.52*** (0.000)	0.31 (0.331)
Crisis	—	—	0.31 (0.218)	0.54* (0.06)	−0.49 (0.831)	0.31 (0.23)	−0.23 (0.266)	0.24 (0.325)	−0.38* (0.057)	0.10 (0.659)	0.15 (0.515)	0.66* (0.021)
IMF	0.72 (0.130)	1.04* (0.046)	—	—	—	—	−0.85* (0.032)	−0.09 (0.82)	−0.54 (0.15)	0.02 (0.953)	−0.41 (0.24)	−0.21 (0.609)
N	214		799		799		994		1009		653	182
Nagelkerke R	0.21		0.138		0.127		0.227		0.227			

Note: Reference category: $^{*}p < 0.1$; $^{**}p < 0.01$; $^{***}p < 0.001$. B = Unstandardised regression coefficients.

are significantly more likely to vote yes or abstain than to vote no. These govern-ments had probably involved the opposition much more in the lawmaking process than they would have done if supported by a parliamentary majority, thus leading to a more consensual decision-making process. Socio-economic policies, for their part, are significantly less likely to trigger a yes than a no (and often an abstention than a no) from the opposition parties – thus supporting the claim that these types of law are more divisive than the others. Finally, we observe that bipartisan or multiparty bills are far more likely to trigger a yes than a no (for almost all parties), but their effect on abstention is not conclusive. On the other hand, we find no support for the effect of the number of committees on voting behaviour, suggesting that more complex laws (at least according to our measure of com-plexity) do not trigger different votes from simple laws.

Conclusions

The opposition's voting behaviour is always pulled between a tendency towards conflict and one towards cooperation. Since the beginning of the crisis, making a choice between these two options has become even more difficult for the opposi-tion because it implies choosing between the need to cooperate with the majority for the nation's sake and the opportunity to weaken an already fragile govern-ment. This contribution has explored how Portuguese opposition parties responded to this dilemma.

Our first conclusion is that, due to the financial crisis, the level of consensus between the government and opposition parties has decreased. The main reason for this decline is the rising number of socio-economic and salient policies – usually more controversial – discussed in parliament. However, both qualitative and quantitative analyses demonstrate a strong variation in the effect of the crisis on the opposition's behaviour across parties. Whereas mainstream and tradition-ally pro-European parties (first the PSD and then the PS) are less adversarial than they would be in normal times, the exact opposite is true for the PCP and PEV, two more radical and Eurosceptic parties. Results are more mixed for the CDS-PP and the BE, which are less extreme in their positive and negative European stances (respectively). These findings thus illustrate the importance of both the exclusion from power and the role external actors play in conditioning the oppo-sition's behaviour in parliament: the European Commission, the European Council, and, since the bailout, the so-called *troika* (EC, ECB and IMF) have played a large role – both positively and negatively – in the current govern-ment–opposition relationship. Finally, we observe a variation across time in the sense that, after the onset, the mainstream opposition parties are more adver-sarial when the possibility of their replacing the government in office increases. Commitment and cooperation do not always prevail over an opposition party's ambition to rule.

The drift towards conflict, however, is not just a prerogative of the opposition. Self-calculation might have been crucial to Sócrates' decision to present a fourth austerity package to parliament without involving opposition parties in the drafting. A similar dynamic seems to have happened with the new PSD/CDS majority government, when a package of austerity measures to be implemented from 2013 onwards was negotiated with the *troika* without consulting the PS (which, in response, felt free to vote against the budget for 2013). Again, by the end of the bailout in 2014, the same government was accused of negotiating fiscal policies with the EU and the IMF behind the scenes. The alleged lack of dialogue with the opposition by both Portuguese prime ministers illustrates that the decision of the opposition parties to vote against or in favour of governmental initiatives may not depend exclusively on their own preferences. It is also contingent on the governing parties' willingness to collaborate.

Acknowledgements

This contribution is the result of a common work. Nonetheless, Elisabetta De Giorgi is particularly responsible for the first and fourth sections, Catherine Moury for the third and fifth, and João Pedro Ruivo for the second section.

Notes

1. The PSD (Social Democratic Party) and the CDS-PP (Democratic and Social Centre – People's Party) are centre-right parties belonging to the European Popular Party. Despite its brief drift to a populist Eurosceptic stance in the 1990s, the CDS has been ideologically closer to European Christian democracy.
2. The parliamentary left in Portugal is composed of three parties: the PCP (the Portuguese Communist Party), the PEV (the left Ecologist Party), and the BE (the Left Bloc, a libertarian left party). The PCP and the PEV usually join together in a pre-electoral coalition (CDU), but split up again in parliament.
3. This argument is clearly supported in Portugal, which had already experienced two financial crises that pushed the country into asking for international financial assistance from the IMF in 1978–79 and in 1983–85. Those interventions, like the current one, triggered political instability and early elections. In two of the three cases, the parliamentary opposition played a crucial role in the government's fall, while in 1983 the government resigned after controversies both within the PSD and with its coalition partner, the CDS. Interestingly, majority coalition governments represented the solution after each fall in order to ensure the legitimacy of the hard policy packages to be implemented under the IMF terms.
4. Face-to-face interviews with 25 former ministers and deputies, January 2013.

5. The Socialists' policy positions, as measured by the policy proposals contained in party manifestos (Volkens et al., 2011), have become closer to those of the parties on their right than on their left.
6. Here we are following Leston-Bandeira (2004).
7. For further details, see the category list of the Comparative Policy Agendas Project at http://www.comparativeagendas.org
8. The analysis was also run with a dummy measuring the effect of the dramatic increase in interest rates (January 2010), which did not have any additional impact on opposition behaviour.
9. For the PCP: after the crisis, the odds of voting yes rather than no decreased by 15 per cent (1−0.85). For the PEV, these odds decreased by 62 per cent (1−0.38).

References

Carammia, M., & De Giorgi, E. (2011, September). *Just empty words? Issue competition in Italy between rhetoric and legislative behaviour.* Paper presented at the Italian Political Science Association Annual Meeting, Palermo, Italy.

Conti, N., & De Giorgi, E. (2011). Euroscetticismo solo a parole? Lega Nord e Rifondazione comunista, tra retorica e comportamento istituzionale. *Rivista Italiana di Scienza Politica, 41*(2), 265–290.

Costa Lobo, M., & Magalhães, P. (2011). Room for manoeuvre: Euroscepticism in the Portuguese parties and electorate (1976–2005). *South European Society and Politics, 16*(1), 81–104.

Dahl, R. (Ed.). (1966). *Political oppositions in western democracies.* New Haven, CT: Yale University Press.

De Giorgi, E. (2011). L'opposition parlementaire en Italie et au Royaume Uni: Systémique ou axée sur les enjeux? *Revue Internationale de Politique Comparée, 18*(2), 93–113.

De Giorgi, E., & Marangoni, F. (2009). The first year of Berlusconi's fourth government: formation, characteristics and activities. *Bulletin of Italian Politics, 1*(1), 87–109.

Di Palma, G. (1977). *Surviving without governing.* Berkley: University of California Press.

Duverger, M. (1954). *Political parties.* (B. North & R. North, Trans.). London: Methuen.

European Commission. (2008). *Communication from the Commission to the European Council. A European Economic Recovery Plan.* Retrieved from http://ec.europa.eu/economy_finance/publications/publication13504_en.pdf

European Council. (2009). *Council recommendation to Portugal with a view to bringing an end to the situation of an excessive government deficit.* Retrieved from http://ec.europa.eu/europe2020/pdf/nd/edp2013_portugal_en.pdf

Flanagan, T. (2001). The uneasy case for uniting the right. *Fraser Institute Occasional Papers: Public Policies Sources, 53*, 3–23.

Hooghe, L., Marks, G., & Wilson, C. (2004). Does left/right structure party positions on European integration? In G. Marks & M. Steenbergen (Eds.), *European integration and political conflict* (pp. 120–140). Cambridge: Cambridge University Press.

Leston-Bandeira, C. (2004). *From legislation to legitimation. The role of the Portuguese parliament.* London: Routledge.

Lewis-Beck, M. S. (1988). *Economics and elections: The major western democracies.* Ann Arbor: University of Michigan Press.

Magalhães, P. (2012). After the bailout: Responsibility, policy, and valence in the Portuguese legislative election of June 2011. *South European Society and Politics, 17*(2), 309–327.

Moury, C., & De Sousa, L. (2011). Comparing deputies' and voters' support for Europe: The case of Portugal. *Portuguese Journal of Social Science, 10*(1), 23–41.

Mújica, A., & Sánchez-Cuenca, I. (2006). Consensus and parliamentary opposition: The case of Spain. *Government and Opposition, 41*(1), 86–108.

Rose, R. (1984). *Do parties make a difference?* London: Macmillan Press.

Sartori, G. (1966). Opposition and control: Problems and prospects. *Government and Opposition, 1*(2), 149–154.

Sitter, N. (2001). The politics of opposition and European integration in Scandinavia: Is Euro-scepticism a government–opposition dynamic? *West European Politics, 24*(4), 22–39.

Sitter, N. (2002). *Opposing Europe: Euro-scepticism, opposition and party competition* (SEI Working Paper No. 56 and OERN Working No. Paper 9). Brighton: Sussex European Institute, University of Sussex.

Stecker, C. (2011, September). *Voting patterns of the parliamentary opposition in Germany*. Paper presented at the Italian Political Science Association Annual Meeting, Palermo, Italy.

Szczerbiak, A., & Taggart, P. (2003, March). *Theorising party-based Euro-scepticism: Problems of definition, measurement and causality*. Paper presented at the European Union Studies Association International Conference, Nashville, TN.

Taggart, P. (1998). A touchstone of dissent: Euroscepticism in contemporary West European party systems. *European Journal of Political Research, 33*(3), 363–388.

Volkens, A., Lacewell, O., Lehmann, P., Regel, S., Schultze, H., & Werner, A. (2011). *The manifesto data collection*. Manifesto Project (MRG/CMP/MARPOR). Berlin: Wissenschaftszentrum Berlin für Sozialforschung.

Government–Opposition Dynamics in Spain under the Pressure of Economic Collapse and the Debt Crisis

ANNA M. PALAU, LUZ MUÑOZ MÁRQUEZ and
LAURA CHAQUÉS-BONAFONT

Government–opposition relations in Spain have been long characterised by a high level of consensus and cooperation. The question analysed here is whether the economic crisis initiated in 2008 has created unprecedented levels of conflict in the political system or whether opposition parties have maintained a cooperative strategy oriented to influence far-reaching policy decisions. Results illustrate that patterns of consensus have decreased significantly since the outbreak of the crisis, and this is partly explained by the rising amount of legislation with socio-economic content, variations in the government's popularity, and the type of government. The analysis also shows that the crisis has increased the incentives of opposition parliamentary groups to oppose European Union legislation, especially among left parties.

Introduction

Following the outbreak of the world financial crisis in 2008, the economic situation in Spain changed dramatically. The economy, which until that time had been enjoying moderate economic growth and government surplus, was plunged into a deep economic recession, with rising levels of unemployment and increasing public debt. In the wake of the recession and collapse of the country's housing market, José Luís Rodríguez Zapatero's socialist government implemented severe austerity measures aimed at reducing state spending and limiting the public sector deficit. Cutbacks in social welfare programmes, pension and labour market reforms were implemented so the government failed to fulfil an important part of its electoral promises. After the socialist electoral defeat in 2011, Mariano Rajoy's conservative government continued to implement policies to curb spending and to control the state deficit. The conservatives launched a major reform of the labour market and financial system and raised taxes, contradicting some of their ideological principles and electoral commitments. In adhering to the recommendations of the EU and other international institutions and by adopting these austerity plans, both governments assumed high political risks in terms of re-election. Indeed, the measures implemented have given rise to considerable political controversy and social mobilisation in Spain, and to unprecedented levels of criticism directed towards European institutions.

The question analysed here is the extent to which the economic crisis has transformed government–opposition relations in Spain. As in other advanced democracies, such as Italy (Cazzola, 1974; Di Palma, 1977), the UK (Rose, 1980), the US (Adler & Wilkerson, 2013; Rose, 1984) and Germany (Rose, 1984; Saalfeld, 1990), government–opposition relations in Spain are characterised by a high level of consensus and cooperation (Capo, 1994; Mújica & Sánchez Cuenca, 2006). Yet to what extent has this consociational behaviour been affected by changes to the social, political and economic context? Is government–opposition consensus immune to the economic crisis? Or, on the contrary, does the crisis represent an opportunity for opposition parties to undermine the government's position, creating unprecedented levels of conflict in the political system? To answer these questions, the patterns of consensus in the Spanish parliament between 2001 and 2012 are examined, considering as explanatory variables the type of government (minority or majority), the socio-economic content of legislation, fluctuations in the government's popularity, and the extent to which the legislative measures are defined by EU institutions. The analysis is based on the final voting pattern for all organic laws and the validation votes for all decree-laws passed in the Spanish parliament during this period.

The following section introduces the theoretical framework and the hypotheses to be tested. The third section outlines the data and methodology used in the analysis. The fourth section describes the changes in government–opposition dynamics in Spain between 2001 and 2012. The fifth explains which variables account for these changes and the last part summarises the main conclusions to be drawn from the analysis.

Theoretical Framework and Hypotheses

Opposition behaviour is central to an understanding of the dynamics of representative democracies. Voting for or against policy decisions is informative about partisan controversy and dissent, providing relevant information about the functioning of democracy (Dahl, 1966; Hix, 2013). Despite this, most studies have focused their attention on the analysis of the output of the legislative process and the spatial location of political parties on policy issues, tending to neglect the analysis of the opposition as a political actor (Mújica & Sánchez Cuenca, 2006; Parry, 1997). Scholars now have excellent exogenous measures of spatial location of parties (Benoit & Laver, 2007; Klingemann, Volkens, Bara, & Budge, 2006), but these analyses do not explain the extent to which these estimated locations translate into revealed behaviour in the most important arena of representative democracy (Petrocik, 1996; Poole, 2005).

A large set of studies analyses voting behaviour in parliaments by considering political parties' tactical choices based on two contrasting options: conflict or cooperation. The *adversarial model* suggests that opposition parties adopt a distinct position from the party in office following a strategy based on conflict (Rose, 1980). Partisanship is considered the driving force in politics, and opposition groups are supposed to behave tactically, emphasising disagreements and confrontation in order to weaken the incumbent government and to gain office. From this perspective, the more a party and its electorate assign relevance to an issue, the more costly it will be to behave consensually (Cazzola, 1974; De Giorgi, 2011; Green-Pedersen, 2007; Jenkins, 2010; Rose, 1984). Opposition behaviour can be expected to be more in conflict on highly visible, politicised issues affecting basic citizens' rights, such as same-sex marriage or abortion, and on economic and social issues, where parties represent different ideological positions and socio-economic interests. For these issues it is hard to justify any shift from the initial party position in the face of the electorate, which is liable to generate conflict and confrontation that persists over time (Mújica & Sánchez Cuenca, 2006).

By contrast, the *consensual model* suggests that parties agree on fundamental issues and that opposition parliamentary groups cooperate with the government to participate in important policy decisions. Parties are in opposition as they are out of government, but they are not necessarily in constant disagreement with the government (Norton, 2008). The parliament is considered a venue for expressing partisan or ideological divisions but it is also an operational governing body oriented to solving problems (Adler & Wilkerson, 2013). This means that parliamentary representatives do not always view choices in purely partisan terms but choose to cooperate on important issues that must be solved even at the risk of suffering electoral consequences. On issues of national interest affecting the whole electorate, such as defence or terrorism, consensus is expected to be high and a problem-solving perspective more likely (Adler & Wilkerson, 2013; Rose, 1984).

As Moury and De Giorgi (2014) argue in the Introduction to this comparative work, because of the characteristics of the actual economic crisis, the dilemma between opting for conflict or cooperation has become particularly acute. In line with the consensual model, in a context of severe economic crisis, opposition parties tend to maintain and even strengthen the pattern of cooperative relations with the government in order to influence far-reaching policy decisions on economic and social issues (Adler & Wilkerson, 2013). By contrast, the adversarial model suggests that in a context of economic crisis voters are more likely to withdraw support from the incumbent government, increasing the opposition's incentive to mobilise popular discontent using a strategy based on conflict (Lewis-Beck, 1988). That is, the economic crisis provides a unique opportunity for opposition political parties to weaken the incumbent government, increasing their possibility of winning power at the next elections. Accordingly, the first hypothesis can be defined as follows:

H1: If the adversarial model holds true, government–opposition relations in Spain should have become increasingly controversial, especially regarding socio-economic issues; by contrast, if the consensual hypothesis holds true, government–opposition relations should have maintained their traditional character based on consensus.

Parliamentary behaviour is shaped, to a large extent, by formal institutions and the type of government (see, for example, Cazzola, 1974; Dahl, 1966; Duverger, 1951; Hix, 2013; Mújica & Sánchez Cuenca, 2006; Pasquino, 1995; Sartori, 1966). In general, it is expected that governments have fewer incentives to seek agreement with opposition parties when they hold a majority of seats. In Spain, this was the case of the governments of the *Partido Popular* (PP) from 2000 to 2004 (with José Maria Aznar as president of the government) and from 2011 to the present (under Mariano Rajoy). Consensus becomes more likely with minority governments, mainly because the incumbent needs the support of other parties to pass the budget and legislation. For the period analysed here, this was the case of Zapatero's socialist government (PSOE),[1] which always governed in a minority (from 2004 to 2011). During the first legislature (2004–8), the PSOE headed a minority government with the support of the far left (*Izquierda Unida* [IU] and *Iniciativa per Catalunya Verds* [ICV]) and *Esquerra Republicana de Catalunya* (ERC), while after 2008 this formal, stable support was diluted into specific and punctual alliances with left and regional political parties. Accordingly, the second hypothesis can be defined as follows:

H2: During minority governments, consensus is higher than under majority governments.

In line with Moury and De Giorgi, government–opposition dynamics are strongly related to the government's popularity and the risk of electoral defeat. An extensive body of research has reported that crisis conditions tend to undermine citizens' support for incumbents (Browne, Frendreis, & Gleiber, 1986; Diamond, Linz, & Lipset, 1989). The magnitude of the electoral impact is correlated with the depth of the crisis experienced in the pre-electoral period measured in terms of variations in exchange rates, gross domestic product (GDP) and/or inflation (Remmer, 1991). In this context, the incentives for the opposition parties to attack the government and to engage in a more adversarial strategy increase as they set about undermining the already low popularity of the government.

In 2008, following Zapatero's re-election, 21 per cent of citizens considered the government's performance to be 'bad' or 'very bad', while four years later, at the end of the legislature, this percentage had risen to 58 per cent. Similarly, the government's popularity declined constantly after the PP won the 2011 general elections, with 66 per cent of Spanish citizens expressing their disapproval of government reforms in 2013 (CIS Barometer, 2013). These falling levels of government popularity are strongly related to the economic crisis ushered in around 2008, characterised by unprecedented levels of complexity and intensity (Barreiro, 2011; Ortega & Peñalosa, 2012; Reinhart & Rogoff, 2009). Unemployment rates have risen more than 15 per cent since the beginning of the crisis, from 9 per cent of the workforce in 2007 to 22 per cent in 2011 and 27 per cent in 2013. The Spanish economy entered recession in 2009, with a 4 per cent negative growth rate, while rising public and private debt levels led to a serious sovereign debt crisis. This poor economic performance and the social consequences of the policy measures adopted to combat the crisis seriously undermined the popularity of incumbent governments. As a result, the third hypothesis can be defined as follows:

H3: Parliamentary consensus falls as the popularity of the incumbent decreases.

Finally, the present economic crisis, in contrast to previous ones, is characterised by the fact that it is being managed in a context of multilevel governance, where most economic policy instruments are in the hands of EU institutions (Hooghe & Marks, 2001). The delegation of decision-making powers to the EU and the creation of European monetary union have meant that most policy measures implemented to overcome the crisis have been prescribed or recommended by external actors. The reform of the Spanish Constitution to cap budget deficit in 2011, the reform of the pension system in 2011 or the provision of rescue loans to the Spanish banks in 2012 are some examples. Existing research has analysed extensively the importance of the strategic interaction between political parties in an attempt to understand the impact of Europe on domestic policies, considering both the role of EU-sceptical extreme parties (Hooghe & Marks, 2009; Kriesi et al., 2008) and the incentives for mainstream political parties to politicise EU issues (Green-Pedersen, 2012). It is argued that pro-European mainstream parties are more likely to cooperate with the incumbent government when policies adopted at the domestic level adhere to EU recommendations. By contrast, Eurosceptic parties have few incentives to collaborate with the incumbent government, especially in relation to highly Europeanised issues (Hooghe, Marks, & Wilson, 2004; Sitter, 2001, 2002; Szczerbiak & Taggart, 2003).

Party positions on European integration influence the politicisation of EU affairs but formal rules also affect to what extent they are the object of parliamentary debates (Bergman & Damgaard, 2000; Karlas, 2012; Raunio, 2005; Strøm, Müller, & Bergman, 2003; Winzen, 2012). In the case of Spain, the parliament plays only a marginal role in relation to EU affairs (it being the executive that intervenes in the agenda-setting and decision-making process) and just a small percentage of directives are finally debated in the *Congreso de los Diputados* (Palau & Chaqués-Bonafont, 2012). Moreover, there are no Eurosceptic parties. No political party has questioned Spanish membership of the EU and public opinion has historically been supportive and enthusiastic of Europeanisation (Closa, 1995; Díez Medrano, 2003, 2007; Sánchez, 1999; Szmolka, 1999). Accordingly, the fourth and final hypothesis can be defined as follows:

H4: Government and opposition are more likely to collaborate on EU-related issues than they are on domestic affairs.

Data and Methodology

This analysis of government–opposition dynamics draws on a database created by the Spanish Policy Agendas Project[2] containing information about the final voting patterns for all the *organic laws* and the validation votes for all the *decree-laws* passed by the Spanish parliament between 2001 and 2012. A total of 104 organic laws and 169 decree-laws are analysed and coded. The approval of organic laws requires an absolute majority in Congress and they are limited to the regulation of certain issues, these being the exercise of fundamental rights and public liberties, the general electoral system, the approval of regional statutes (*Estatutos de Autonomía*), and other procedures considered in the Spanish Constitution, including the regulation of the Constitutional Court, the Ombudsman (*Defensor del Pueblo*) and the states of alert, emergency or siege. Organic laws represent 13 per cent of all the laws passed in Spain in the period 2001–12.

Decree-laws are provisional regulatory acts passed by the executive in case of extraordinary or urgent necessity, or when exceptional circumstances impede the implementation of ordinary legislative procedures. In accordance with the Spanish Constitution, decree-laws cannot affect the regulation of basic state institutions, rights, duties, and liberties of citizens, the *Estatutos de Autonomía*, or the general electoral system. Decree-laws have to be submitted for debate and voting by the entire Congress within 30 days of their promulgation. The Congress has to adopt a specific decision on their ratification or revocation in the same period, with the option of processing them as executive bills. Decree laws represent 22 per cent of all the laws passed in Spain in the period 2001–12.

The database contains information about the total number of votes and the specific votes cast by each parliamentary group (positive, negative, abstentions and absences). Data about the total number of votes are available on the Spanish Congress webpage (www.congreso.es), while information concerning the voting behaviour of each parliamentary group is available only on request and for the period 2001–12,[3] which is why this analysis was circumscribed to this period. This database draws on those previously created by the Spanish Policy Agendas Project, which provide information about the specific issue addressed by the legislative measure, the legislature, year, month, title, author of the initiative, and the EU content of organic laws and decree-laws (Chaqués-Bonafont, Palau, & Baumgartner, forthcoming; Chaqués-Bonafont, Palau, & Muñoz, 2014). Legislation is considered to be *Europeanised* if it is totally or partially defined by an EU-binding regulatory act (Brouard, Costa, & Köning, 2011; Palau & Chaqués-Bonafont, 2012).

The level of conflict and consensus is measured using the index developed by Capo (1994). This index of consensus is based on the following formula:

$$IC = \frac{vf}{n*v/N}$$

where vf corresponds to the total number of positive votes cast for a law, n is the number of deputies in the governing party, v is the total number of votes, including positive and negative votes as well as abstentions, and N is the size of the assembly (350). The index can be interpreted as follows: if the index has a value of one, the incumbent party does not obtain support from any other parliamentary group; whereas if the index has a value greater than one, the incumbent obtains support from other groups: the more support it receives, the higher the value.

To analyse the impact of minority–majority governments, in line with Mújica and Sánchez Cuenca (2006), the difference in the number of seats between the incumbent and the main opposition party is taken into account. The analysis of the impact of legislative issue type draws on the 19 topics identified by the Comparative Agendas Project. A dummy, with a value of one if the legislation is related to topic 1 (economy), 3 (health), 5 (labour), 6 (education), 13 (social policy), and 15 (commerce and banking) and zero otherwise,[4] is used to determine whether socio-economic measures are more open to conflict than other issues. Finally,[5] government's popularity is measured in accordance with the barometer published by the *Centro de Investigaciones Sociológicas* (http://www.cis.es) and, more specifically, according to the responses given to the following question: How do you evaluate the government's performance: very good, good, bad, very bad?

Government–Opposition Dynamics in Spain

Previous analysis of government–opposition dynamics based on the analysis of organic laws (Mújica & Sánchez Cuenca, 2006) illustrates that consensus has been the dominant pattern in Spanish politics. During the country's first legislature, in the transition to democracy, 97 per cent of organic laws were passed with a positive vote from the main opposition party. This percentage subsequently fell to 44 per cent during Felipe González's first term in office (1982–86), when the socialists enjoyed an absolute majority. It then rose again during the minority governments of Felipe González (1993–96) and José Maria Aznar (1996–2000), when the percentage reached 76 and 77 per cent, respectively. Overall, between 1979 and 2001, the government and the main opposition party were in agreement on 71 per cent of the organic laws passed in the Spanish parliament.

This pattern was reversed between 2001 and 2012. The consensus declined during José Maria Aznar's majority government (PP), when 61 per cent of organic laws were passed with a positive vote from the main opposition party, but also during Zapatero's first minority government (PSOE), when the percentage fell to 55 per cent. The latter rate can be explained by the controversial policy reforms implemented by the socialists in areas such as education, immigration or the disputed reform to the Catalan Statute introduced during this period. The level of consensus rose again during the socialists' second legislature (to 69 per cent), when although conflict was high in relation to certain issues (for example, the reform of the abortion act), a significant number of organic laws concerning issues on which party conflict is very low (for example, the ratification of the Lisbon Treaty) were introduced. By contrast, the level of consensus fell dramatically after 2011, with only 37 per cent of organic laws having been passed with the support of the socialist party, the lowest level of consensus since the transition to democracy. In the case of decree-laws,[6] the level of consensus rose during Zapatero's first minority government (the percentage of these laws passed with the support of the main opposition party increased from 55 per cent in the period 2001–4 to 64 per cent for the period 2004–8). After 2008, following the outbreak of the economic crisis, the level of consensus fell to 43 per cent during Zapatero's second legislature and to 28 per cent during that of Rajoy (2011–12).

The index of consensus (Figure 1) and the mean percentage of positive and negative votes (Figure 2) corroborate this decline in parliamentary consensus over time, and especially since 2011, when the PP began to govern with an absolute majority and important reform measures aimed at tackling the economic crisis were passed. If a consideration is given to both organic laws and decree-laws, the results show that the level of consensus was higher during the socialist legislatures – the mean percentage of positive votes increased from 42 per cent during Aznar's absolute majority (2001–4) to 55 and 53 per cent during Zapatero's first and second legislatures, respectively. Consensus, however, declined markedly in 2012, with Rajoy taking office, as the mean percentage of positive votes fell from 53 to 26 per cent, while that of negative votes increased from 12 to 52 per cent.

As Table 1 illustrates, there has also been considerable variation in the voting behaviour of parliamentary groups across legislatures. On the one hand, the two main state-wide political parties – the PSOE and the PP – adopt different

Figure 1: Index of Consensus: Organic Laws and Decree-laws (2001–12)

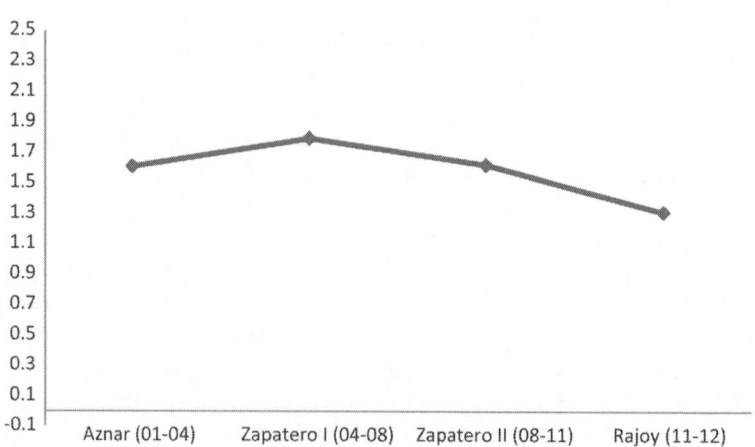

Figure 2: Mean Percentage of Positive and Negatives Votes of Opposition Parliamentary Groups over Time: Organic Laws and Decree-laws (2001–12)

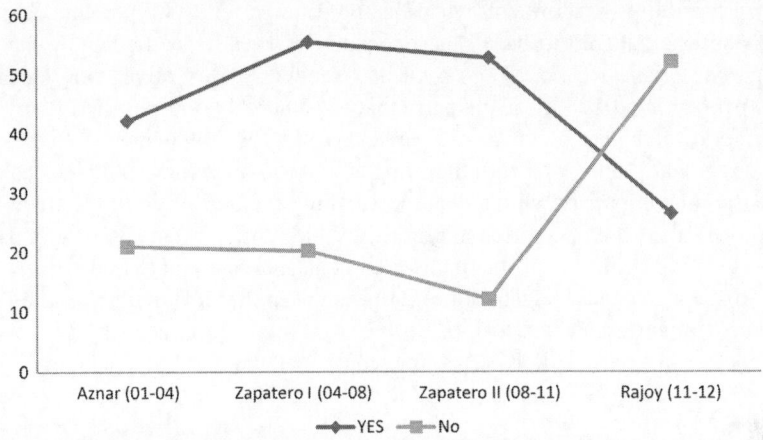

strategies: overall the PP gives more support to the incumbent political party than is the case with the PSOE. The mean percentage of positive votes cast by the PP during the two legislatures governed by the PSOE was 53 per cent. By contrast, the mean percentage of positive votes cast by the PSOE between 2001 and 2004

Table 1: Mean Percentage of Positive and Negative Votes by Different Parliamentary Groups: Organic Laws and Decree-laws (2001–12)

		Legislature			
		Aznar (2001–4)	Zapatero I (2004–8)	Zapatero II (2008–11)	Rajoy (2011–12)
PSOE	Yes	44.6	93.1	97.2	27.5
	No	24.8	0.3	0.1	59.3
PP	Yes	87.6	53.5	52.6	96.1
	No	0.2	24.5	12.3	0.1
CIU	Yes	65.2	71	65.7	49
	No	5.9	4.9	1.4	27.9
PNV	Yes	31.6	60.4	60	28.1
	No	11	5	17.2	23.2
ERC	Yes		70		
	No		5		
IU*	Yes	22.4	70.7	42.5	6.6
	No	23.5	6.3	29.9	59.7
CC	Yes	45.8	44.8		
	No		0.5		
UPyD	Yes				38.4
	No				48.6

*IU votes with ERC and ICV in the legislature 2008–11 and with ICV and Chunta Aragonesista in 2012.

(during the Aznar government) was just 45 per cent. The decline in socialist support for the incumbent party was even more marked during 2012, the first year of the Rajoy government, when this percentage fell to 27 per cent. In fact, this pattern is adhered to by all the opposition parties, in particular by the far-left party *Izquierda Unida*. With a mean percentage of negative votes standing at 60 per cent in 2012, this is the party that most fiercely opposes the PP government, followed by the socialists (59 per cent) and UPyD (49 per cent). In the case of the regional political parties, their opposition to government policies has also increased in comparison with levels recorded in previous legislatures, albeit less intensively than the opposition expressed by the other parliamentary groups. In the case of CIU, the mean percentage of negative votes increased from 1 per cent in Zapatero's last legislature to 28 per cent in 2012. By contrast, the PNV presented much greater opposition to the legislation introduced by the PSOE, especially in the period 2008–11 (17 per cent). Yet, the mean percentage of negative votes of the PNV increased significantly with Rajoy in power (23 per cent).

Analysis and Results

To analyse the extent to which changes in the index of consensus can be explained by the type of legislation under debate (that is, the socio-economic content of the proposed measure), the type of government, variations in government's popularity and the degree of Europeanisation (whether the measure involves EU-related legislation), an ordinary least squares regression (OLS) regression was conducted (see the following equation). Differences between the parliamentary groups were analysed using the same regression equation but considering the mean percentage of positive votes cast by each group as the dependent variable. In the case of the PP and the PSOE, the fact of their being in office or in opposition was also taken into consideration.

$$IC = C + \beta_1 SocEcoIssues + \beta_2 SeatDif + \beta_3 GovUnpop + \beta_4 EUcontent + \varepsilon$$

where: IC = Capo's (1994) index of consensus for all organic laws and decree-laws passed between 2001 and 2012; $SocEcoIssues$ = unity if organic laws and decree-laws involve socio-economic issues, zero otherwise; $SeatDif$ = difference in the number of seats between the government and the main party in opposition; $GovUnpop$ = government's unpopularity measured by the percentage of citizens considering the government's performance as being 'bad' or 'very bad'; and $EUcontent$ = unity if organic laws and decree-laws are totally or partially defined by an EU binding regulatory act.

As Figure 3 illustrates, the amount of socio-economic legislation has increased in recent years in parallel with the worsening of the economic crisis. During Aznar's last government (2001–4) and Zapatero's first legislature (2004–8), legislation tackling socio-economic issues accounted for 38 and 35 per cent of the total (considering both organic laws and decree-laws),

Figure 3: Percentage of Socio-economic Legislation, Unemployment Rate, Variations in the Popularity of the Government and Index of Consensus (2001–12)

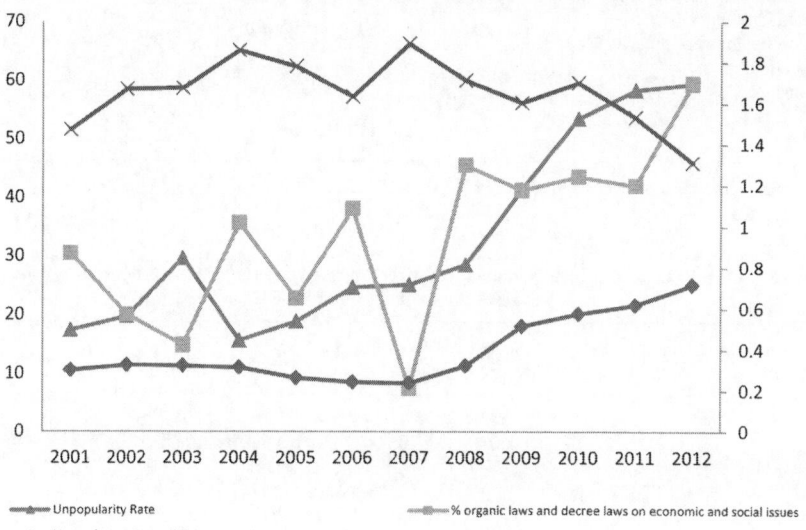

respectively. Between 2008 and 2011, this percentage rose to 45 per cent, and in 2012, under Rajoy, it reached 65 per cent. This increase was especially high in the case of decree-laws, which, since 2008, have accounted for 89 per cent of all socio-economic legislation. The regression results (Table 2)[7] show that the consensus on socio-economic issues was lower than that on other issues – the index of consensus fell by 0.2 when legislation involved socio-economic measures. This variable is negative and statistically significant for all the opposition groups (Table 3). Only when the PP and the PSOE are in office are they more likely to give support to economic and social measures, because they initiate legislation – 71 per cent of all organic laws and decree-laws were introduced by the government.

Although the index of consensus on economic and social issues declined in Zapatero's second legislature and immediately after the PP took office, conflict has always been higher in relation to socio-economic measures than in relation to that of any other policy area (Figure 4). Moreover, following the outbreak of the crisis, consensus declined in relation to all policy areas, not just in relation to socio-economic measures. Overall, in relation to *H1*, these results demonstrate that opposition parliamentary groups tend not to opt for a strategy based on cooperation to tackle the crisis, nor do they adopt a problem-solving perspective. On the contrary, conflict concerning socio-economic affairs has always been high and it has increased since the outbreak of the crisis, and at present it is especially marked since the PP won an absolute parliamentary majority at the 2011 general elections.

Table 2: OLS Regression Results: Variables Affecting the Index of Consensus

Economic and social issues	$-0.209^{***}(0.000)$
Seat differences	$-0.004^{***}(0.000)$
Government unpopularity	$-0.004^{**}(0.006)$
EU content	$-0.046(0.365)$
Constant	1.996
R-Square	0.168
N	273

Note: $p < 0.10$; $^*p < 0.05$; $^{**}p < 0.01$; $^{***}p < 0.001$.

Table 3: OLS Regression Results: Variables Affecting the Decision of Parliamentary Groups to Vote Yes for Legislation (2001–12)

Group	Economic and Social Issues	Seats Differences	Government Unpopularity	EU Content	Intercept	R-Square	N
PSOE	-8.115*	-1.154***	0.164***	3.197	108.766	0.575	248
	(0.02)	(0.000)	(0.000)	(0.329)			
PSOEGov	0.774	–	0.121***	-0.504	90.89	0.239	146
	(0.245)		(0.000)	(0.424)			
PSOEOpo	-22.098**	–	-0.232	7.112	51.383	0.1	102
	(0.01)		(0.312)	(0.363)			
PP	-12.969**	0.781***	0.006	-6.45	47.528	0.267	248
	(0.006)	(0.000)	(0.962)	(0.142)			
PPGov	2.281	–	0.206***	-0.417	82.932	0.34	102
	(0.075)		(0.000)	(0.724)			
PPOpo	-22.543**	–	0.048	-9.926	62.711	0.077	146
	(0.004)		(0.833)	(0.179)			
CIU	-12.828**	-0.167+	-0.244+	-7.049	86.294	0.089	248
	(0.008)	(0.065)	(0.076)	(0.121)			
PNV	-13.84**	-0.57***	0.012	3.081	71.337	0.137	248
	(0.014)	(0.000)	(0.939)	(0.561)			
IU	-13.375**	-0.755***	-0.37**	-3.45	86.074	0.329	248
	(0.004)	(0.000)	(0.005)	(0.421)			

Notes: We have only considered those groups with parliamentary representation during the whole period under analysis (2001–12). For those parties that only have parliamentary group in one legislature, such as ERC or UPyD, it is not possible to control for the impact of some variables in the model, for example the type of government. In the case of IU, the parliamentary group includes ERC and ICV in the legislature 2008–11 and ICV and Chunta Aragonesista in 2012.
$^+p < 0.10$; $^*p < 0.05$; $^{**}p < 0.01$; $^{***}p < 0.001$.

The regression results also illustrate that as the difference between the number of seats held by the government and the main opposition party increases, the index of consensus decreases. As Table 3 illustrates, this variable is statistically significant and the coefficient negative for all parliamentary groups – as the difference in the number of seats increases, the mean percentage of positive votes for legislation falls – with the exception of the PP, which presents a positive coefficient because it always enjoyed an absolute majority during the period of analysis (Figure 5).[8] In the case of IU, support was higher in Zapatero's first legislature

Figure 4: Index of Consensus (2001–12): Differences by Type of Legislation

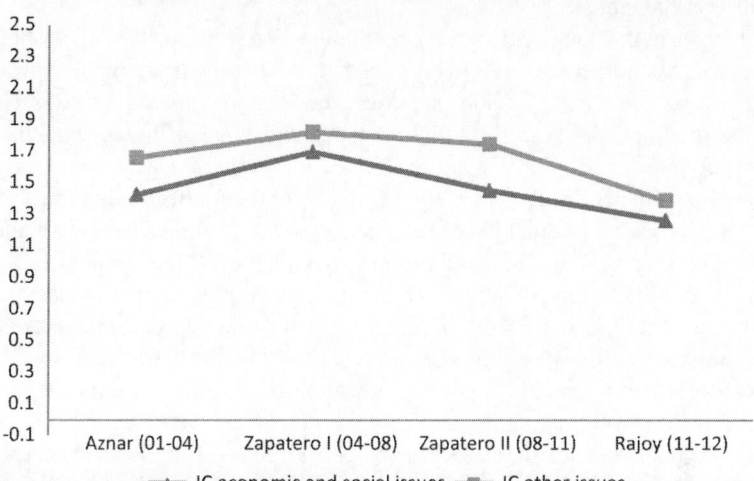

as the socialists relied on the support of this party, as well as that of ERC, to govern. Following the electoral reverse suffered by IU in the 2008 general elections, the mean percentage of positive votes of this group fell, initiating a period of greater opposition to government legislation. Overall, these results corroborate

Figure 5: Mean Percentage of Positive Votes for Legislation Considering Seats Difference and Parliamentary Groups

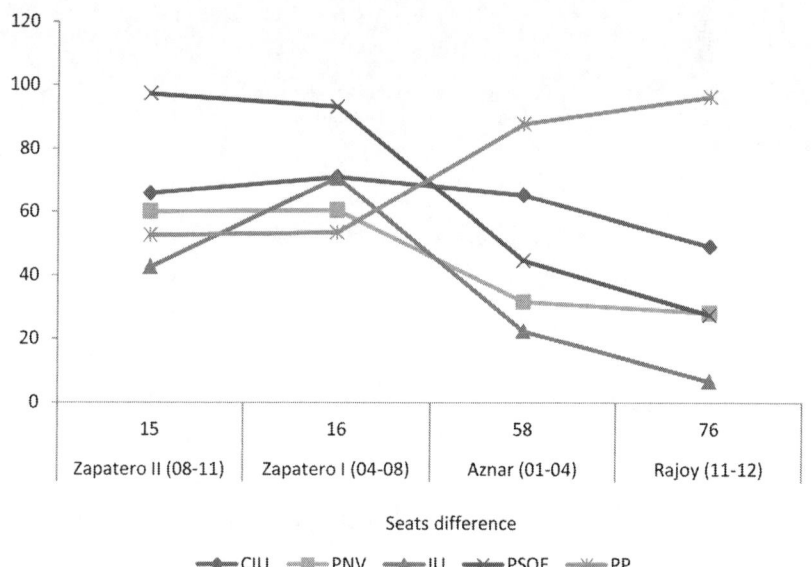

H2: the type of government significantly affects the pattern of consensus in the Spanish parliament.

Changes in the popularity of the government also seem to affect the pattern of consensus: as the percentage of the public that believes the government to be doing a 'bad' or 'very bad' job increases, the index of consensus falls. Given that the likelihood of winning office is especially high in the case of the two state-wide parties (the PP and the PSOE), it is particularly interesting to analyse how changes in the popularity of the incumbent affect the voting behaviour of these two parties that have alternated in power over the last few decades in Spain. The results show that as the popularity of the PP government falls, the PSOE is less likely to give support to the incumbent government (a statistically significant negative coefficient). This accounts for the high percentage of negative votes cast by the PSOE in relation to the legislation introduced by Rajoy, especially regarding socio-economic legislation (Figure 6). By contrast, fluctuations in the popularity of the Aznar government did not significantly affect the voting behaviour of the PSOE in the period 2001–4, basically because the popularity of the conservatives remained high, with the exception of the year 2003, coinciding with citizen discontent with Spain's involvement in the Iraq war (Figure 3).

In the case of the PP, by contrast, the regression results illustrate that when this party is in opposition and the popularity of the PSOE is low, it is more likely to vote in favour of legislation. But the coefficient is not statistically significant. Moreover, although the positive coefficient could suggest that the PP voting behaviour is designed to overcome the crisis by adopting a strategy of cooperation, if the same regression is run considering only socio-economic legislation, the coefficient becomes negative. As Figures 6 and 7 show, the PP gave

Figure 6: Mean Percentage of Positive Votes, Negative Votes and Abstentions of the PSOE to Socio-economic Legislation

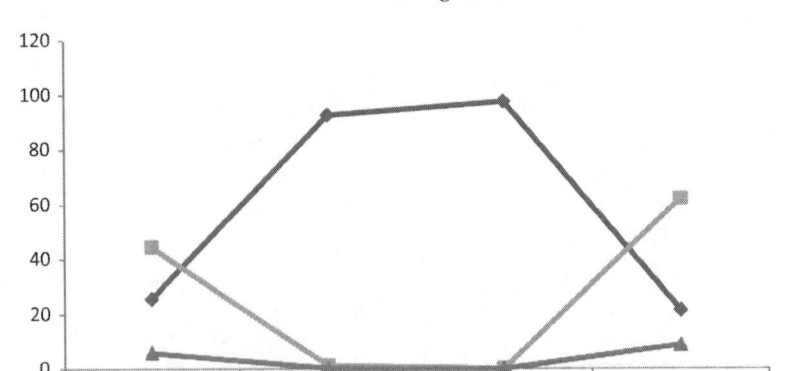

Figure 7: Mean Percentage of Positive Votes, Negative Votes and Abstentions of the PP to Socio-economic Legislation

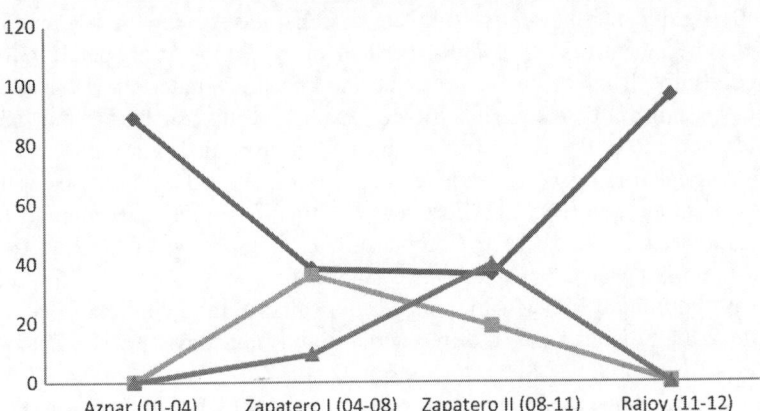

more support to the socio-economic legislation passed by Zapatero designed to tackle the crisis than the PSOE have given to date to the measures adopted by Rajoy, although the PP basically adopted a strategy based on abstention: the mean percentage of PP abstentions in votes on socio-economic legislation increased from 9 per cent during Zapatero's first legislature to 40 per cent in his second term in office. The PP gave support to some of the measures introduced by the PSOE to tackle the crisis, for example legislation designed to facilitate credit access for businesses and families, but in other important areas of policymaking, such as the labour market reform of 2010 or the package of economic measures introduced in 2008 to promote economic activity, the PP abstained.

A possible interpretation of this abstention is that the conservative party did not want to give support to the measures passed by the socialists but neither did they want to appear to be in disagreement with EU institutions, given that the majority of these policies were introduced in line with EU recommendations. The PP strategy therefore was that of not taking a public stance so as to maximise utility in the eyes of voters and EU institutions, given the likelihood of their winning office in the next elections.[9] The analysis of PP abstentions shows that during Zapatero's second legislature the abstention rate was higher on EU-related legislation (42 per cent) than it was on domestic measures (36 per cent). As for the other parliamentary groups, CIU and IU present a regression coefficient that is negative and statistically significant, indicating that they behave less consensually when the unpopularity of the incumbent government is high, this being especially true of IU. As for the PNV, the coefficient is not statistically significant because of the high percentage of abstentions recorded by this group in votes concerning policies adopted by the Rajoy government.

In the case of EU-related measures, the results show that the index of consensus declines when legislation is of this nature; and while the coefficient is not statistically significant, its negative sign suggests that the economic crisis may have reduced the incentives for Spanish parliamentary groups to cooperate on EU-related affairs. It might be the case that the crisis has undermined the output-based legitimacy that has historically explained the support from public opinion and the political parties in Spain for European integration. As Jones (2009) argues, the crisis has sapped support for the euro, undermined trust in EU institutions, especially the European Central Bank, and in so doing, it has also exposed a weakness in the output-oriented legitimacy of the EU. In this sense the crisis would appear to have significantly affected one of the pillars that has traditionally upheld support for European integration in Spain: economic growth and a reduction of the difference in living standards between Spain and the rest of Europe (Díez Medrano, 2007).

As a result, some political parties, especially those to the left (for example, the IU), which were already critical of the social consequences of the Maastricht Treaty and the Constitutional Treaty, have started to express serious concerns about the turn of events in specific EU policy areas. As Figure 8 illustrates, IU is the parliamentary group that expresses greatest opposition to EU-related legislation, especially to measures tackling socio-economic issues. Other parties similarly oppose EU-related legislation, but they adopt different strategies over time. When the PP and the PSOE are in power, these two parties never oppose EU-related socio-economic legislation. However, when they are in opposition, they adopt a completely distinct voting behaviour. In the case of the PSOE, during the Rajoy government the mean percentage of negative votes increased to 55

Figure 8: Mean Percentage of Negative Votes to Legislation With and Without EU Content by Political Party (2001–12)

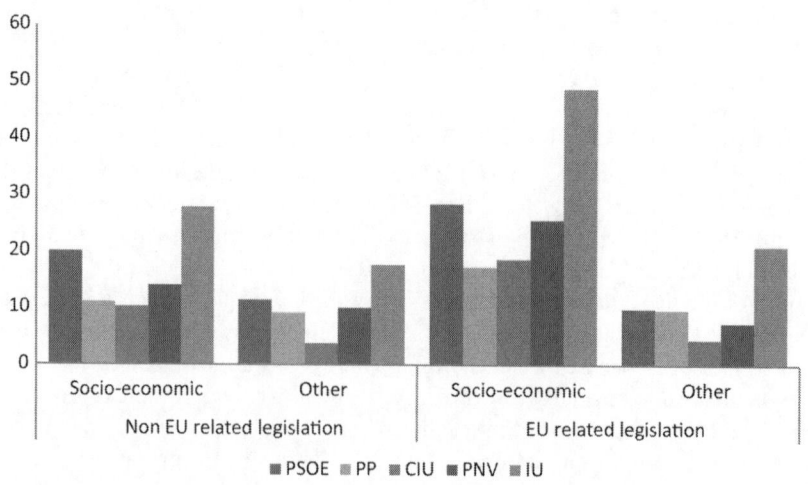

per cent. In the case of the PP, on the other hand, when in opposition, and especially during Zapatero's last legislature, the party opposition to EU-related legislation was lower (27 per cent of negative votes) and, as outlined above, adopted a strategy based primarily on abstention. In the case of IU, its opposition to this type of legislation has always been high, presenting a mean percentage of negative votes that has consistently been above 50 per cent during both Zapatero's last legislature and the first two years of the Rajoy government.

Overall, and as a direct result of the economic crisis, Spanish parties, and especially those to the left, have not called into question Spanish membership of the EU, but they now have additional incentives to pay attention to EU affairs as a means of demonstrating their disagreement with EU decisions and also of responding to shifting public opinion perceptions of European integration. According to a recent poll, Spanish citizens are increasingly distancing themselves from national institutions and at the same time becoming more critical of EU institutions. A large majority of Spaniards (86 per cent) think that if EU institutions continue to implement the policies that have been developed to manage the crisis, the EU will no longer be 'useful'. Moreover, 84 per cent believe that the EU's economic policies respond more to German interests than they do to those of other countries, and 94 per cent consider it necessary to reform EU institutions (CIS Barometer, 2013).

Conclusions

The economic crisis has contributed significantly to the reduction in the level of consensus between government and opposition in Spain. Indeed, the consensus index has fallen since the outbreak of the crisis during Zapatero's second legislature (2008–11), and the level is now particularly low under Mariano Rajoy's government (2011–12). This dynamic is partly explained by the rising amount of legislation with socio-economic content introduced to tackle the crisis; however, the type of government should also be taken into account to understand patterns of conflict and cooperation. The results reported here illustrate that consensus increases when the incumbent is in need of the support of opposition parties to pass legislation. Opposition support for legislation was higher during the minority governments of Zapatero than it was during the absolute majority enjoyed by Aznar, and is now especially low following the absolute majority won by Rajoy.

The opposition's voting behaviour has also been more adversarial following the outbreak of the crisis because the measures adopted to tackle it have resulted in a marked decline in the popularity of the incumbents. The results illustrate that as the popularity of the government falls the opposition tends to behave less consensually because the possibilities of winning office or improving electoral performance increase. Overall, it seems that the opposition opts for a strategy based on conflict so as to weaken the government rather than for a strategy based on cooperation. The rise in the mean percentage of negative votes in all parliamentary groups during the Rajoy legislature or the strategic use of absten-tion by the PP during Zapatero's last legislature serves to corroborate that problem-solving strategies do not drive politics under the pressure of economic collapse and debt crisis.

Finally, the results illustrate that government–opposition dynamics are influ-enced by the context of multilevel governance in which many decisions to manage the crisis are taken. Although there are no Eurosceptic parties in Spain's political system, opposition to legislation with EU content has been high during the period of analysis, especially in relation to socio-economic measures and among parties to the left. Economic decline has increased the incentives of opposition parliamentary groups to oppose EU-related legislation as an indication of their disagreement with EU decisions but also to respond to shifting public opinion perceptions of European integration.

Acknowledgements

This research was undertaken by the Grup d'Anàlisi Comparada de l'Agenda Política (Spanish Policy Agendas Project) with the institutional support of the AGAUR and the Ministerio de Economía y Competitividad.

Funding

This work was supported by Agència de Gestió d'Ajuts Universitaris i de Recerca (AGAUR) [grant number SGR 536]; Ministerio de Economía y Competitividad [grant number CSO-2012-31214].

Notes

1. Full names of all abbreviated parties in the text are the following: PSOE, Partido Socialista Obrero Español; PP, Partido Popular; CIU, Convergència i Unió; PNV, Partido Nacionalista Vasco; ERC, Esquerra Republicana de Catalunya; IU, Izquierda Unida; CC, Coalición Canaria; UPyD, Unión Progreso y Democracia.
2. The legislative databases created by the Spanish Policy Agendas Project have been coded manually by two coders in accordance with the methodology applied by the Comparative Agendas Project, which identifies 19 major legislative fields and 247 subcategories (Chaqués-Bonafont, Palau, & Baumgartner, forthcoming).

3. Information about the total number of votes cast (positive, negative, absences and abstentions) is provided for all the decree-laws and organic laws. However, information about the voting behaviour of each parliamentary group is missing in the case of 15 decree-laws and eight organic laws.
4. Subcategory 1523 (natural disasters and accidents) is not considered in topic 15 as it is not directly related to economic and social issues.
5. Although the impact of the economic and fiscal crises is analysed here, the regression model does not specifically include a variable to operationalise the variable 'crisis' by considering, for example, unemployment rates or changes in GDP, because this variable was found to be highly correlated with government popularity and therefore introduced serious multicollinearity into the model.
6. No previous analysis of consensus has been undertaken for decree-laws. Mújica and Sánchez Cuenca (2006) considered only organic laws and so it is not possible to compare these results with the situation prior to 2001.
7. The Durbin–Watson test indicates that there is no autocorrelation, the variance inflation factor (VIF) and tolerance test that there is no multicollinearity and the Breusch–Pagan/Cook–Weisberg test that there is no heteroskedasticity in the regression models.
8. The regression equations that consider the differences between the PP and the PSOE when in office and when in opposition do not take into account the difference in the number of seats. In the case of the PP, this is because when the PP was in opposition the PSOE was always a minority government and the PP always governed with an absolute majority; in the case of the PSOE, this is because this variable is highly correlated with the variable measuring changes in the popularity of government, which introduces a serious multicollinearity problem in the regression.
9. Unlike other countries, such as Norway, Spanish parliamentary rules do not allow representatives to vote either in favour or against legislation (Rasch, 1995). However, there is no single way of interpreting the meaning of such an abstention. For example, its effects are strongly related to the type of government. When the governing party has an absolute majority, abstention cannot prevent the adoption of legislation, but when there is a minority government, abstention may mean that the governing party does not satisfy the quorum required to pass legislation and, therefore, depending on the position taken by other parliamentary groups, it may have a veto effect.

References

Adler, S., & Wilkerson, J. D. (2013). *Congress and the politics of problem solving*. Cambridge: Cambridge University Press.
Barreiro, B. (2011). In the whirlwind of the economic crisis: Local and regional elections in Spain. *South European Society and Politics, 17*(2), 281–294.
Benoit, K., & Laver, M. (2007). Estimating party positions: Comparing expert surveys and hand coded content analysis. *Electoral Studies, 26*, 90–107.
Bergman, T., & Damgaard, E. (Eds.). (2000). Delegation and accountability in European integration: The Nordic parliamentary democracies and the European Union. Special issue of the *Journal of Legislative Studies, 6*(1).
Brouard, S., Costa, O., & Köning, T. (2011). *The Europeanization of domestic legislatures: The empirical implications of the Delors' Myth in nine countries*. Studies in Public Choice. New York, NY: Springer.
Brown, E., Frendreis, J., & Gleiber, D. (1986). The process of cabinet dissolution: An exponential model of duration and stability in western democracies. *American Journal of Political Science, 30*, 628–650.
Capo, J. (1994). Oposición y minorías en las legislaturas socialistas. *Revista Española de Investigaciones Sociológicas, 66*, 91–113.
Cazzola, F. (1974). *Governo e opposizione nel parlamento italiano*. Milan: A. Giuffrè.
Chaqués-Bonafont, L., Palau, A., & Baumgartner, F. (forthcoming). *Agenda dynamics in Spain*. London: Palgrave.
Chaqués-Bonafont, L., Palau, A., & Muñoz, L. (2014). Policy promises and governmental activities in Spain. In C. Green-Pedersen & S. Walgrave (Eds.). *Tracing political attention: A novel approach to comparative politics* (pp. 183–200). Chicago, IL: Chicago University Press.
CIS Barometer (2013). http://www.cis.es/cis/opencm/ES/1_encuestas/estudios/ver.jsp?estudio=14010

Closa, C. (1995). Spain: The Cortes and the EU – a growing together. *The Journal of Legislative Studies*, *1*(3), 136–150.

Dahl, R. (Ed.). (1966). *Political oppositions in western democracies*. New Haven, CT: Yale University Press.

De Giorgi, E. (2011). L'opposition parlementaire en Italie et au Royaume Uni: Systémique ou axée sur les enjeux? *Revue Internationale de Politique Comparée*, *18*(2), 93–113.

Diamond, L., Linz, J., & Lipset, S. M. (Eds.). (1989). *Democracy in developing countries: Latin America*. London: Adamantine Press.

Díez Medrano, J. (2003). *Framing Europe: Attitudes to European integration in Germany, Spain, and the United Kingdom*. Princeton, NJ: Princeton University Press.

Díez Medrano, J. (2007). La opinion pública española y la integración europea. In F. Morata & G. Mateo (Eds.), *España en Europa – Europa en España (1986–2006)* (pp. 205–233). Barcelona: Fundació CIDOB.

Di Palma, G. (1977). *Surviving without governing*. Berkeley: California University Press.

Duverger, M. (1951). *Political parties: Their organization and activity in the modern state*. Paris: Armand Colin.

Green-Pedersen, C. (2007). The growing importance of issue competition: The changing nature of party competition in western Europe. *Political Studies*, *55*(4), 608–628.

Green-Pedersen, C. (2012). A giant fast asleep? Party incentives and the politicisation of European integration. *Political Studies*, *60*, 115–130.

Hix, S. (2013). *Government–opposition or left–right? The institutional determinants of voting in legislatures* (Working Paper). London: London School of Economics.

Hooghe, L., & Marks, G. (2001). *Multi-level governance and European integration*. Oxford: Rowman & Littlefield.

Hooghe, L., & Marks, G. (2009). Postfunctionalist theory of European integration: From permissive consensus to constraining dissensus. *British Journal of Political Science*, *39*(1), 1–23.

Hooghe, L., Marks, G., & Wilson, C. (2004). Does left/right structure party positions on European integration? In G. Marks & M. Steenbergen (Eds.), *European integration and political conflict* (pp. 120–140). Cambridge: Cambridge University Press.

Jenkins, S. (2010). Examining the influence over roll call voting in multiple issue areas: A comparative US state analysis. *Journal of Legislative Studies*, *16*(1), 14–31.

Jones, E. (2009). Output legitimacy and the global financial crisis: Perceptions matter. *Journal of Common Market Studies*, *47*, 1085–1105.

Karlas, J. (2012). National parliamentary control of EU affairs: Institutional design after enlargement. *West European Politics*, *35*(5), 1095–1113.

Klingemann, H., Volkens, A., Bara, J., & Budge, I. (2006). *Mapping policy preferences II: Estimates for parties, elector and governments in central and eastern Europe, European Union and OECD 1990–2003*. Oxford: Oxford University Press.

Kriesi, H., Grande, E., Lachat, R., Dolezal, M., Bornschier, S., & Frey, T. (2008). *West European politics in the age of globalization*. Cambridge: Cambridge University Press.

Lewis-Beck, M. S. (1988). *Economics and elections: The major western democracies*. Ann Arbor: University of Michigan Press.

Moury, C., & De Giorgi, Elisabetta (2014). Introduction: Conflict and consensus in Parliament during the economic crisis. *Journal of Legislative Studies*, DOI:10.1080/13572334.2014.939564.

Mújica, A., & Sánchez Cuenca, I. (2006). Consensus and parliamentary opposition: The case of Spain. *Government and Opposition*, *41*(1), 86–108.

Norton, P. (2008). Making sense of opposition. *The Journal of Legislative Studies*, *14*(1–2), 236–250.

Ortega, E., & Peñalosa, J. (2012). The Spanish economic crisis: Key factors and growth challenges in the Euro area. *Documentos Ocasiones*, 1304. Banco de España.

Palau, A. M., & Chaqués-Bonafont, L. (2012). Europeanization of legislative activity in Spain. In S. Brouard, O. Costa, & T. Köning (Eds.), *The Europeanization of domestic legislatures. The empirical implications of the Delors' Myth in nine countries* (pp. 173–196). Studies in Public Choice. New York, NY: Springer.

Parry, G. (1997). Opposition questions. *Government and Opposition*, *32*(4), 451–461.

Pasquino, G. (1995). *L'opposizione*. Bari: Laterza.

Petrocik, J. R. (1996). Issue ownership in presidential elections, with a 1980 case study. *American Journal of Political Science*, *40*(3), 825–850.

Poole, K. T. (2005). *Spatial models of parliamentary voting*. Cambridge: Cambridge University Press.

Rasch, E. (1995). Parliamentary voting procedures. In H. Döring (Ed.), *Parliaments and majority rule in western Europe* (pp. 488–527). New York, NY: St. Martin's Press.

Raunio, T. (2005). Holding governments accountable in European affairs: Explaining cross-national variation. *Journal of Legislative Studies*, *11*(3–4), 319–342.

Reinhart, C., & Rogoff, K. S. (2009). The aftermath of financial crises. *American Economic Review*, *99*(2), 466–472.

Remmer, K. (1991). The political impact of economic crisis in Latin America in the 1980s. *The American Political Science Review*, *85*(3), 777–800.

Rose, R. (1980). *Do parties make a difference?* London: Macmillan.

Rose, R. (1984). *Understanding big government*. London: Sage.

Saalfeld, T. (1990). The West Bundestag after 40 years: The role of parliament in a party democracy. In P. Norton (Eds.), *Parliaments in western Europe*. London: Frank Cass.

Sánchez, I. (1999). El déficit democrático en la Unión Europea. In I. Llamazares & F. Reinares (Eds.), *Aspectos políticos y sociales de la integración europea* (pp. 94–116). Valencia: Tirant lo Blanch.

Sartori, G. (1966). European political parties: The case of polarized pluralism. In J. LaPalombara & M. Weiner (Eds.), *Political parties and political development* (pp. 137–176). Princeton, NJ: Princeton University Press.

Sitter, N. (2001). The politics of opposition and European integration in Scandinavia: Is Euroscepticism a government–opposition dynamic? *West European Politics*, *24*(1), 22–39.

Sitter, N. (2002). Cleavages, party strategy and party system change in Europe east and west. *Perspectives on European Politics and Society*, *3*(3), 425–451.

Strøm, K., Müller, W. C., & Bergman, T. (Eds.). (2003). *Delegation and accountability in parliamentary democracies*. Oxford: Oxford University Press.

Szczerbiak, A., & Taggart, P. (2003, March). *Theorising party-based Euroscepticism: Problems of definition, measurement and causality*. Paper presented at the European Union Studies Association International Conference, Nashville, TN.

Szmolka, I. (1999). *Opiniones y actitudes de los españoles ante el proceso de integración europea*. Opiniones y Actitudes, 21. Madrid: CIS.

Winzen, T. (2012). National parliamentary control of European Union affairs: a cross-national and longitudinal comparison. *West European Politics*, *35*(3), 657–672.

An Emerging Divide? Assessing the Impact of the Euro Crisis on the Voting Alignments of the European Parliament

STEFANO BRAGHIROLI

The euro crisis is increasingly affecting the political debate in the European Union. Exogenously determined power shifts and institutional changes have been imposed on a number of member states. These measures and the direct intervention of external stakeholders in the key realms of domestic politics pose a serious challenge to both the EU's cohesiveness and its democratic nature. This study looks at how the voting dynamics and the government/opposition-like alignments in the European Parliament are affected by the ongoing crisis. It highlights the balance of partisan and nationally driven factors behind legislators' choices related to the management of the crisis. To capture the impact of the crisis-related debate on the actors' cohesiveness and alignments, two sets of vote-based analyses are conducted. This analysis proves that the main determinant of legislators' alignments in crisis-related debates is membership of the eurozone, while the explanatory potential of factors such as ideology and partisanship appears residual.

Introduction

Since 2009 the international financial crisis has hit the EU and has dramatically affected its functioning and political dynamics. If one looks at the way the discourse on the eurozone crisis has affected the political debate in the EU together with the way it has been constructed in the transnational context, a variety of positions can be identified, largely determined by the domestic perspective through which the crisis is framed and contextualised. According to a number of observers, the perpetration of these dynamics, reflecting exogenous direct interventions on key realms of domestic politics, might determine a drift of European unity along geo-territorial, ideological, or economic lines (Verney, 2009).

A number of recent studies show that these cleavages are likely to undermine the effectiveness of a common European strategy. Elgström, Bjurulf, and Johansson (2001) stress the growing rift between Mediterranean and northern European/ continental member states; while Zimmer, Schneider, and Dobbins (2005) stress the differences between the 'old' and the 'new' member states from central and eastern Europe (CEE). Others highlight the divergence of interests between members of the eurozone and other member states (von Hagen, Schuknechtd, & Wolswijk, 2009).

As the representative of Europe's citizens, the European Parliament (EP) is likely to be influenced in its activities by these exogenous factors. A brief look at the deliberations held in the EP on the ongoing crisis shows that the crisis-related parliamentary debate emerges as a cross-cleavage and highly divisive factor. Given the high salience of the issue at stake, these dynamics might pose a serious challenge to the alleged process of 'normalisation' for the EP and to the coherence of its party groups[1] and delegations of members of the EP (MEPs).

So far, only limited empirical research related to the ongoing crisis has been conducted from an EP perspective, while most of the attention has been devoted to the Council and the European Commission (EC) or to national debates.

The present study aims to assess to what extent and in which direction the debate on the ongoing crisis affects voting dynamics in the EP and its distinctive government/opposition-like alignments. Given its multidimensional nature combined with its direct representativeness, EP deliberations are likely to reflect and amplify the cleavages that characterise the European and domestic debates on the crisis. The positions of the different party groups and delegations of MEPs are likely to reflect distinct ways of understanding the crisis and different degrees of support and opposition for the measures proposed at both the domestic and European levels.

In an attempt to assess the impact of the crisis-related debate on the voting dynamics and alignments, this analysis will 'map' the voting behaviour of the MEPs in the current parliamentary term, with an eye on the sixth EP for comparative purposes.

This analysis will first perform a vote-based comparative assessment of party groups' cohesiveness, coherence, and coalition patterns, within the current and previous EP terms (2004–12). It will distinguish the votes according to their crisis-related nature. In the second part of the analysis, the impact of the ongoing debate on legislators' collective voting through government/opposition-like alignments will be assessed using hierarchical cluster analysis.

The study proceeds as follows: after discussing, in the next section, the conceptual framework and the actors involved – the research strategy of the study – cases and methods will then be defined in the section following this. The penultimate section will discuss the empirical results of the comparative analysis while the final section will present some concluding considerations and discuss potential broader implications.

Conceptual Framework of the Study

As the initial concerns emerged about a possible sovereign debt crisis in the eurozone by virtue of the Greek government debt crisis in 2009, the European institutions (in particular the EC) proved weak in the management of this critical situation. The debate has focused on inter-state negotiations between the member states directly hit by the crisis and the most stable economies under the auspices of a *troika* formed by the EC, the European Central Bank (ECB) and the International Monetary Fund (IMF). Concerns intensified in early 2010 when other southern European member states experienced increasing difficulties in placing their sovereign assets, leading EU governments to agree on a series of financial support measures such as the European Financial Stability Facility (EFSF) and the European Stability Mechanism (ESM). Supplementary to these political measures, in September 2012 the ECB announced potentially free unlimited support for all eurozone countries involved in the debt crisis. The activism of the ECB sparked strong criticism among net contributors such as Germany, Austria, the Netherlands, and the Nordic countries.

Accordingly, a wide variety of positions concerning the management of the crisis can be identified in the EU arena. Several factors concur with the divisive temptations of the member states, as the crisis is framed and understood differently in different national contexts.

The European Parliament and the Euro Crisis

While denying the domestic relevance of the ongoing debate on the crisis seems to be out of the question, the balance of domestic and European factors that determine the EP voting stance on it still needs to be clarified. The parliamentary debate on the euro crisis might represent a useful analytical shortcut to assess and empirically test the impact of nationally salient issues on EP voting dynamics and alignments.

The key reason behind the lack of research on the EP can be attributed to its alleged limited role in this policy area. However, this idea seems to be far from reality for two reasons. First, in light of the recent provisions introduced by the Lisbon Treaty, the EP has gained power exponentially vis-à-vis other EU institutions, while also showing greater activism within the sphere of economic and monetary affairs. Worth noting further is the EP's role in the emerging governance of the eurozone; in scrutinising the implementation of the ESM and monitoring the actions of the EC, the Euro-group of eurozone finance ministers, and the ECB (Hix, 2013). Although the EP's activism is not necessarily fully reflected in the EP's prerogatives, its substantial influence on the debate is increasing. Moreover, its limited formal powers in the field grant the EP more *liberté de manoeuvre* than the Council and the EC. Second, the EP is the only directly elected EU institution. Accordingly, it is not only the sole legitimate representative of EU citizens at the supranational level, but, given its nature and composition, it is also more likely to reflect their attitudes in voting dynamics. Given its multinational and politically diverse character, partisan–ideological cleavages emerge in the EP not only between, but also within, national delegations. The EP represents a direct channel that conveys national inter-party politics to the European political arena. This perspective challenges the realist idea of EU member states as unitary actors; an assumption better fit by other 'executive' institutions of the EU. In the light of this, it seems worthwhile to assess the relative weight of European partisanship and national interests inside the different delegations at the EP level.

Economic and monetary affairs have represented a key area of interest for the EP. The debates on the ongoing crisis are highly prioritised both in the plenary and in the Committee for Economic and Monetary Affairs Meeting (ECON). Key issues under debate include the implementation of the ESM, financial assistance to the highly indebted member states, creation of Eurobonds, and a more central role for the ECB. According to Hix (2011), while in 2009 a stable coalition between the EPP and ALDE groups dominated the committee, the third semester (July–December 2010) saw a noticeable increase in the appearance of the 'grand coalition' (up to 81 per cent of votes), marking the highest level in the period 2004–10. Does this evolution mirror the voting dynamics in the plenary when crisis-related votes are at stake?

Resolutions, reports, and recommendations represent the most frequent legislative and non-legislative activities of the EP. Worth mentioning are the recent debates on 'Financial, economic and social crisis: recommendations concerning the measures and initiatives to be taken' (20 October 2010), 'Motions for resolutions – establishing a permanent crisis mechanism to safeguard the financial stability of the euro area' (16 December 2010), 'Financial, economic and social crisis: measures and initiatives to be taken' (6 July 2011), and 'Motions for resolutions – feasibility of introducing stability bonds' (15 February 2012).[2] The latter deals with the creation of Eurobonds, a collective bond system for pooling the sovereign debt of eurozone member states. Although this is a non-legally binding resolution, the position of the parliament is nonetheless important, given its power of scrutiny (Hix, 2013).

The majority of MEPs from the EPP, Socialist, ALDE and Greens voted in favour of the resolution. The vote passed by 515 in favour, to 125 against, with 52 abstentions. However, 29 EPP MEPs from Germany and Sweden voted against, and 19 ALDE MEPs, mostly from Germany, abstained. There was also opposition from the ECR and most MEPs in GUE-NGL and EFD (Hix, 2013). Furthermore, votes held on 6 July 2011 highlighted a partisan/ideological rift between mainstream and non-mainstream party groups and an interest-based rift between eurozone and non-eurozone delegations (the Swedish, British, Polish, and Danish delegations). In both cases mentioned the result of the vote denotes a lack of internal voting coherence in the three major parties. The following quotes are excerpts from the debates surrounding the above-mentioned votes:

> Thomas Ulmer (EPP, Germany) – I voted against this report because it turns budgetary consolidation by the Member States on its head and contains the usual flowery Communist dross about inter-State transfers.

> Carl Haglund (ALDE, Finland) – I, Carl Haglund, decided to abstain from supporting the resolution on the feasibility of introducing stability bonds following my firm conviction that a system of permanent joint liabilities

for sovereign debt is no solution for the eurozone. In addition to this, there are a number of issues concerning moral hazard, wrong incentives, impacts on the interest rates and legal constraints that, as yet, have not been appropriately tackled in my view.

George Sabin Cutaş (S&D, Romania) – I voted for the European Parliament Resolution on establishing a permanent crisis mechanism to safeguard the financial stability of the euro area, given that this kind of mechanism has become a necessity in the current economic and financial crisis. I also support this resolution as it calls for the mechanism to be inspired by the Community method, which involves decision making at a common European level. Having a permanent crisis mechanism is beneficial to all Member States, including those which have not yet adopted the euro, given the interdependency among Europe's economies.

Charalampos Angourakis (GUE-NGL, Greece) – The war against the workers, the self-employed and small-scale farmers is a strategic choice by the bourgeois governments and the EU in order to support the profitability of capital. The debt and deficit are simply a pretext . . . There is an urgent need for a broader grassroots rally to radically reverse the power correlations for the benefit of the grassroots alliance and to achieve an exit from the EU.

Daniel Hannan (ECR, UK) – Madam President, when I was a teenager, I travelled in what we still thought of as Eastern Europe and I remember being struck, even then, by the paradox that here was a system that nobody believed in. Even the people running it no longer professed, if ever they had, the principles of Marxism–Leninism. Yet one could not see how it was going to end because so many people had a vested interest in the maintenance of the status quo. I had an eerie sense of nostalgia as I listened to the debate this morning. One by one, the pillars that sustained the European ideal have been kicked away and yet we continue to tell ourselves that the answer is more integration, more Europe, monetary and fiscal union, common economic governance, and so on.

As is evident from the quotes above, the EP's stance on the crisis can hardly be defined as unitary as it highlights consistent national and partisan patterns, but also cuts across the traditional alignments. The way in which the debate is framed reflects a wide variety of positions and implies the imperfect juxtaposition of at least two broadly defined factors: nationality and partisanship.

The debate on the continuing crisis represents a relevant and generalisable case study for four reasons. First, it represents a typical cross-cleavage issue of a clear transnational nature affecting all the member states and very diverse strata of the EU's societies. Second, its significance is indisputable given the evident repercussions of the crisis both on societal and on political dynamics. Third, given the different interests at stake and the different ways in which the crisis has affected the member states, inter-state coalitions are emerging when it comes to the definition of the distribution of costs among the actors involved. Fourth, the ideological potential of the debates on the crisis is indisputable, as it implies different political/economic recipes and different winners and losers according to the choices sponsored.

The Voting Dynamics in the European Parliament

Several have claimed the EP's 'normalisation' and increasing comparability with respect to member states' legislatures. This claim, implying a progressive parliamentarisation of the EU, has been generally linked to two phenomena (Hix, Noury, & Roland, 2006). First, since its inaugural direct election in 1979, a gradual but constant increase in the competences and powers of the EP has marked the EU decision-making process. Today, the EP has a wide range of prerogatives somehow comparable to those of most of the legislatures in Europe. The Lisbon Treaty acknowledges the EP's role as equal co-legislator vis-à-vis the Council of Ministers, thereby paving the way for a two-chamber system. Second, a number of scholars (Hix & Noury, 2009) highlight a trend towards higher ideological coherence in EP deliberations at the expense of its consociational nature (Fabbrini, 2005). Hix (2005) and Kreppel (2002) claim that the voting alignments in the EP are more ideologically coherent as a consequence of the generalised introduction of qualified majority voting (QMV).

Whereas wide scholarly attention has been devoted to the normalisation of the EP and the voting behaviour of its members, a very limited amount of analysis has been conducted on the effects of exogenous factors and issue-salience on the trend of normalisation as well as on voting alignments. Concerning the tension between partisan and nationally driven factors, the literature suggests the possibility of two distinct scenarios.

As mentioned above, the remarkable level of voting cohesion reflects the increasingly central role of European party groups as successful aggregators of interests (Hix, 2005). In a study on legislators' preferences, Voeten (2005) claims that 'the European Party Groups are more successful than national parties in swaying MEPs from their stated ideal points' (p. 3). He concludes that '[they] appear capable of swaying MEPs towards their ideal points, thus exerting some amount of control over the policy-making process. All of this is good news for the thesis that the EP has many of the features of a normal parliament' (p. 20). Other studies have highlighted the growing ideological coherence of EP voting alignments. They confirm that a large majority of the votes can be read in light of the group affiliation of an MEP, while only a minority of votes can be explained along national lines.

Other works describe the EP as a weak chamber susceptible to 'multiple influences operating upon its members such as diverse policy preferences, national interests, national party policies, and European party affiliations' (Hix, 2002, p. 688). While acknowledging growing intra-group coherence, the same studies demonstrate the disruptive impact of domestically sensitive votes on legislators. In other words, when domestic pressure is exerted, MEPs tend to vote along national lines – allegedly reflecting some sort of national interest – at the expense of group coherence (Hix, 2002; Kreppel, 2002).

In line with this narrative, a number of realist authors stress the relevance of national interest and claim that the debate on the ongoing European sovereign debt crisis is determined by both the balance of member states' stances and their relative weight. Given the specific domestic significance of the issue, the EP cannot be seen as an independent actor, but MEPs appear subject to the priorities of their respective member states' national interests. As put by Faas (2003), 'bargaining in the Council of Ministers is often very difficult and time-consuming. Once a compromise has been found there, national governments do not want the EP to overturn it. Hence, they put pressure on their MEPs to vote for the compromise, even if that implies voting against the line of their EP party group' (p. 845). Support for these arguments was found in studies analysing domestically sensitive votes such as the election of the EC president (Hix, 1997; Hix & Lord 1996), the enlargement process (Öhlén, 2013), or the treaty reforms (Moravcsik, 1998).

Government and Opposition Dynamics in the European Parliament?

Studies about government–opposition dynamics at the EP level are very rare. Despite widespread scepticism with regard to identifying clear government–opposition dynamics in the EP, in the last decade a number of scholars have begun to speak about the possibility of discerning parliamentary opposition in the EU as part of the normalisation trend. Helms (2008) considers the EC to be the main locus of executive power in the EU. From this perspective, both the EP and the Council can be considered the legislative chambers of the Union. Others consider the EC and the Council as a 'dual executive' (Hix et al., 2006) and accordingly define the EP as the locus of parliamentary opposition (Helms, 2008). Helms also identifies some traditional expressions of parliamentary opposition based on the political role of reasonably coherent groups of MEPs. The EU has traditionally been defined as a consensual system (Costa & Magnette, 2003; Lijphart, 1999). Settembri (2006) and Taylor (1991) maintain that consociational theory explains the overwhelming share of EP voting dynamics defined by a 'giant coalition'. Past studies have also suggested that the decision-making of the EP is characterised by 'grand coalition' alignments. This would confirm the idea of those who affirm that the EP also follows a consensual system. The three main parties vote together, thereby determining a conflict between the mainstream and non-mainstream groups. According to Hix (2005), in the last parliaments the former represent the 'governing parties'. Against this majority, two blocks of opposition can be identified: on the left, the Greens and the radical left, and on the right, the Conservatives and the anti-European parties. Recent studies have problematised this perspective. They claim that MEPs tend to vote more in line with their ideological pattern, thereby eroding 'grand coalition' alignments (Hix, 2003; Kreppel, 2002).

In line with these findings, Braghiroli and Smaldore (2011) have proposed a 'variable-geometry government–opposition model' based on groups' involvement in parliamentary majorities, distinguishing between institutional and political votes. Eurosceptics and the radical left are defined as *opposition parties*, whereas EPP and ALDE are defined as a *governmental coalition*. The Greens are labelled as a *governmental opposition party* as they tend to coalesce only on institutional votes, while they oppose most of the political votes. The Socialists seem to stay at the margins of the *governmental coalition*.

Worth noting is a link between party groups' support for the appointed EC and their belonging to the 'governmental coalition'. Braghiroli and Smaldore (2011) show that one party's support of a 'vote of confidence' for the EC will almost certainly determine that party's inclusion in winning majorities in most of the votes, thereby supporting the EC's 'programme' and emerging as a *sui generis* 'governmental coalition'.

This analysis aims to identify the balance between European/partisan and domestic factors as well as their repercussions for MEPs' collective voting trends and coalition patterns. In light of the arguments presented in the sections above, this study will test a set of four hypotheses patterned after the idea of different, multi-cleavage, and (potentially) intertwined explanatory planes. The following hypotheses, addressing MEPs' voting behaviour and government/opposition-like alignments, call into question both partisan factors (*H1a* and *H1b*) such as the divide between mainstream and non-mainstream forces and the left–right divide, and nationally driven factors (*H2a* and *H2b*) such as the geo-territorial divide or states' participation in EU integration structures such as the euro.

> *H1a: In times of crisis the mainstream parties are more likely to coalesce and behave cohesively on economy-related votes than in 'normal times'; while non-mainstream parties are likely to constitute an opposition block.*

> *H1b: When votes directly related to the crisis are at stake, 'grand coalition' alignments are less likely, given the strong ideological charge attached to the debates, as they imply different political/economic recipes and different winners and losers according to choices sponsored.*

> *H2a: Keeping the other factors constant, in times of crisis the mainstream parties are more likely to be internally cohesive on general economy-related votes than on votes directly related to the crisis, as the crisis is framed and understood differently in the different national contexts in light of different national interests.*

H2b: In votes directly related to the crisis, geo-territorial and interest-based factors are more likely to (re)define government/opposition-like alignments in the EP, while the impact of ideology appears residual and mostly limited to the non-mainstream parties.

Methods, Measures and Techniques

This analysis is based on 33 roll-call votes (RCVs) held between 2009 and 2012 (see the Appendix). A RCV is a vote in which legislators' voting choice is recorded for each individual, identified by name, in the minutes.[3] The study focuses on the parliamentary works of the current and previous EP. To grant the consistency of the votes analysed, only the votes falling into the policy area of 'economic and monetary affairs' were considered as they represent the sole votes directly related to the debate on the crisis. Other votes falling into different areas, only tangentially related to the crisis debate, appear to call into play other policy realms (and different national and political priorities) whose weight in the voting dynamics would be difficult to determine. All the bills included are either resolutions or motions for resolutions[4] and deal mainly with the implementation of the ESM, financial assistance to highly indebted member states, creation of Eurobonds, and the definition of the role of the ECB.

Defining the Roll-call Vote-based Tests

The first part of the analysis implies a comparison of party groups' cohesion in three different voting contexts. Cohesion measures are calculated on the basis of the crisis-related votes (CRISIS sample), the votes dealing with 'economic and monetary affairs' (ECO sample), and all the votes available in the respective EP term[5] (ALL sample). ECO is a subset of ALL, while CRISIS is a subset of both ECO and ALL. The first part of the analysis covers both the current and the previous EP (sixth and seventh EPs), thereby assessing the voting dynamics before and during the crisis. Obviously, the CRISIS sample covers only the current EP.

The measure of groups' cohesion is based on Attinà's agreement index (*AI*). Unlike other measures of groups' coherence, the former has been specifically developed to measure the voting cohesion in the EP and to account also for 'abstentions' (Attinà, 1990). The index is as follows:

$$AI_i = \frac{\max\{Y_i, N_i, A_i\} - \frac{1}{2}[(Y_i + N_i + A_i) - \max\{Y_i, N_i, A_i\}]}{(Y_i + N_i + A_i)}$$

where Y_i denotes the number of 'yes' votes expressed on a given vote (i), N_i the number of 'no' votes and A_i the number of abstentions. The index equals one when all the members of one given group vote together and equals zero when the members are equally divided between all three of these voting options. The average score of the group represents its cohesion measure.

The second part of the analysis implies the empirical definition of the voting clusters of legislators' delegations, accounting for the results of the first analytical step. The procedure adopted implies three successive steps. First, crisis-related bills are identified and selected.[6] Second, for every crisis-related bill considered, legislators' individual voting stances are computed. Third, a final measure of delegations' average voting proximity (*Davp*) is calculated for every national delegation on the basis of each legislator's stance:

$$Davp = \left(\frac{nP - nN}{nP + nN}\right)$$

where *nP* represents the number of positive votes, *nN* the number of negative votes. The final measure ranges from minus one (all affiliated MEPs express a negative vote) to one (vice versa). A score of zero denotes a perfectly split delegation. The closer the two delegations' scores, the more similar their stance on crisis-related votes.

The constellations of actors in the debates are identified according to their delegations' affiliation using cluster analysis on the basis of the computed *Davp* scores. Cluster analysis is a statistical method that groups (or segments) a collection of data rows into 'clusters' (Hartigan, 1975; Zhong & Ghosh, 2003). The data grouped within each cluster are more closely related to one another than those assigned to any clusters that are different. The process of grouping follows the notion of degree of similarity (or dissimilarity) between the individual objects to be clustered.[7] Clustering has been widely used in the social sciences; however, its application to political science is still limited. Webb (2008) and Chae (2010) introduced hierarchical clustering to find groups in political attitude. Spirling and Quinn (2010) used cluster analysis for investigating legislative voting behaviour. Compared with other scaling techniques, clustering has a number of key advantages as it does not require a priori assumptions (for example, NOMINATE) and it shows more than how 'far' various observations are from one another (for example, agglomerative clustering).

Defining the Constellation of Actors and Factors in Crisis-related Votes

This section first comparatively assesses changes in MEPs' collective behaviour when crisis-related votes are at stake, before then discussing the results of the RCV-based hierarchical cluster analysis.

Comparative Assessment of Groups' Cohesion and Alignments

Figures 1 and 2 chart party groups' cohesion in the sixth and seventh EPs. The level of cohesion is calculated according to Attinà's agreement index (1990)

Figure 1: Comparative Internal Cohesion of the Party Groups in the Seventh European Parliament

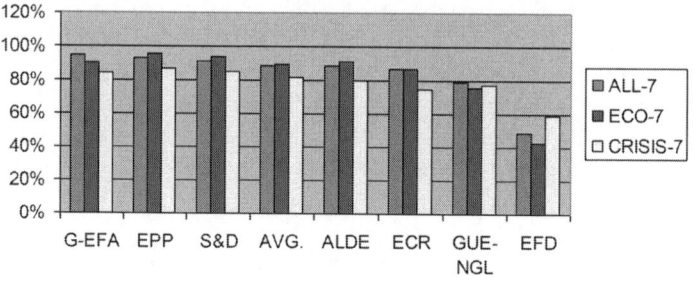

Figure 2: Comparative Internal Cohesion of the Party Groups in the Sixth European Parliament

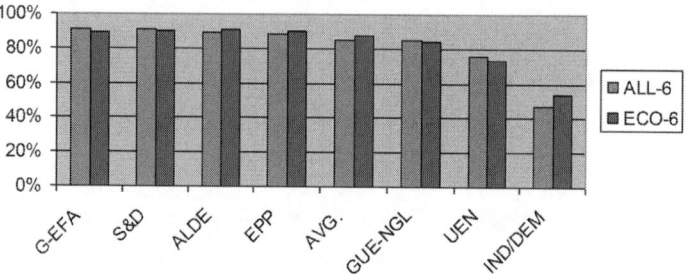

on the basis of three samples of votes defined in the previous section (ALL, ECO, and CRISIS).

Figure 1 represents a generalised trend that involves all the mainstream party groups in the current EP. They all present a structurally high level of cohesion (ALL), higher than 85 per cent, and topping 90 per cent in the case of EPP, S&D, and ALDE. In almost all the cases, the level of cohesion in the ECO votes appears higher than in the ALL sample. This datum, in line with *H1a*, is not only confirmed by the scores of the three main party groups (96 per cent versus 93 per cent for EPP; 94 per cent versus 91 per cent for S & D; and 91 per cent versus 89 per cent for ALDE); but also reflected – although more moderately – by the average EP scores. If one looks at the CRISIS votes, in five out of the seven groups the trend marks a substantial decrease in group coherence, with an average decline of almost 10 percentage points (CRISIS = 82 per cent). In the case of ALDE and ECR, the decrease is higher than 10 percentage points; while in other cases – EPP, Greens, and GUE-NGL – it is more moderate.

The party groups that experience the most substantial drop in the internal cohesion are those that appear more coherent in terms of economic policies (ECO). While, as a result of the crisis, the level of intra-group cohesion in the

ECO votes appears understandably higher than average voting cohesion (ALL), it decreases substantially when it comes to the CRISIS votes. This seems to confirm *H2a* and contradicts the expectation of responsible burden-sharing behaviour involving the mainstream parties. This datum suggests that, while the crisis has determined more cohesive voting attitudes when it comes to general votes on 'economic and monetary affairs', only marginally related to the crisis, this trend is not taking place in the votes that are related more directly to the crisis.

Figure 2 charts the groups' internal cohesion in the sixth EP, before the eruption of the crisis, distinguishing between the ALL and ECO samples. Not surprisingly, also in the sixth EP, the three main party groups (and the Greens) emerge as the most cohesive in both the ALL and ECO samples. On the other hand, average intra-group cohesion has increased in the current term. The phenomenon appears even more relevant when it comes to the ECO votes, where the cohesion of all the mainstream groups grew substantially (EPP +6 percentage points, S&D +4, ALDE +1, G-EFA +2, average +5). The comparative analysis of the sixth EP also confirms *H1a* and *H2a*. When economy-related votes are at stake, a trend towards convergence emerges in line with the idea of sharing responsibilities in difficult times; this trend does not take place in the votes more directly related to the crisis. On the contrary, an opposite trend is possibly emerging, as demonstrated by the decrease in intra-party cohesion in the CRISIS votes.[8]

Figure 3 charts inter-group voting dynamics in the seventh EP as reflected by party groups' comparative participation in winning voting coalitions when crisis-related votes are held. If one looks at the three main party groups, a less cooperative and more ideologically coherent inter-party voting behaviour emerges. In the ALL sample the participation rate in the winning coalitions of the three main party groups equals, respectively, 89 per cent for EPP, 86 per cent for ALDE, and 83 per cent for S&D, thereby confirming that a cooperative voting style among the three main party groups is dominating the dynamics in the EP (*H1a*). As hypothesised (*H1b*), if one looks at the crisis-related votes, a much larger ideological drift emerges between the liberal-conservative and

Figure 3: Party Groups' Participation in Winning Voting Coalitions in Crisis-related Votes (Seventh European Parliament)

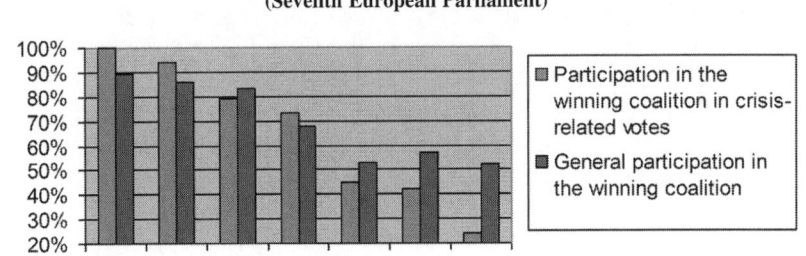

progressive-socialist components. While the S&D group is included in the winning coalitions 79 per cent of the times, the percentage increases to 94 per cent for the ALDE group and even to 100 per cent for the EPP group. The minor party groups face a generalised drop in their participation rate.

This first analytical step, however, suggests that ideologically defined clusters, such as the EP's party groups, do not say much about the actual definition of the opposed voting constellations. Some evidence of this crucial point is represented by the fact that EPP and ALDE – together dominating the winning coalitions – present the least internally coherent voting behaviour in CRISIS votes.

The crisis-related RCVs considered in this analysis deal with three main points: the adoption of the ESM, the creation of Eurobonds, and the definition of a more effective role for the ECB. Although in theory the mainstream party groups have clear ideas about these points (favouring the three measures), on more than one occasion the affiliated MEPs belonging to different national delegations voted in opposite ways. In the final vote on a 'Motion for resolutions – establishing a permanent crisis mechanism to safeguard the financial stability of the euro area' the AI score of S&D, ALDE, and EPP dropped, respectively, to 50, 76, and 88 per cent, thereby confirming *H2a*. Given their national government's opposition to the creation of a Eurobond regime, the German MEPs, who were affiliated both to the EPP and ALDE, voted against the line of their party group.

Clustering MEPs' Delegations

If one thinks of legislators' voting cohesion as a system of communicating vessels, it is reasonable to suppose that as intra-party cohesion decreases, the weight of nationally driven factors increases, as reflected by the coherence of voting blocs patterned after alleged national interest(s). One might expect that as the party groups' (ideological) internal coherence decreases in the CRISIS-related votes, the coherence of inter-state blocs inside the EP grows as a consequence of MEPs' propensity to perform nationally oriented considerations in domestically significant votes. However, what one does not know is according to which criteria national lines cross-cut and according to which patterns national delegations coalesce or oppose each other. As hypothesised in the previous sections, the divide might reflect ideological or geo-territorial dimensions or the degree of participation in the structures of European integration or incorporate different endogenous factors. In order to identify the determinants of these dynamics, a cluster analysis of the 27 national delegations in the EP has been conducted on the basis of the delegations' *Dvap* scores for each of the crisis-related votes taken into consideration.

The dendrogram in Figure 4 charts national delegations' voting patterns in light of the degree of similarity or dissimilarity in their *Dvap* scores. In line with *H2b*, the dendrogram highlights the presence of two geo-territorial macro-clusters and five sub-clusters, including 26 out of 27 national delegations.[9] The key interest-based factor that affects MEPs' national-oriented voting (as

Figure 4: Clustering National Delegations' Voting Attitudes in Crisis-related Votes

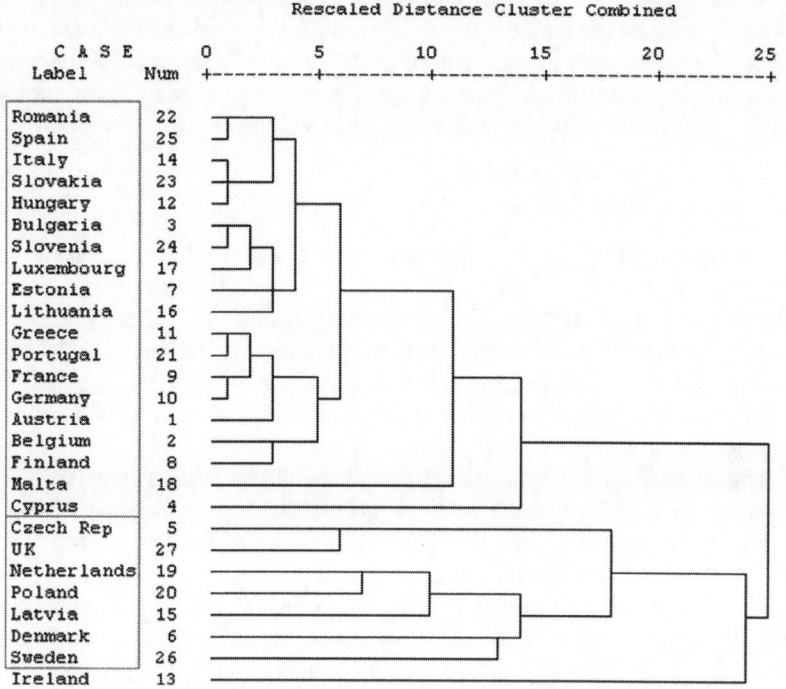

highlighted by the decline in groups' cohesion) and the EP's government/opposition-like alignments is a divide between the eurozone delegations and those that do not participate in the European single currency. The 'Euro cluster' includes 15 out of the 16 computed euro member states, with the exception of the Netherlands.

The second macro-cluster includes six delegations that do not participate in the eurozone, plus the Netherlands. The only non-euro delegations falling in the 'Euro cluster' are those of Romania, Hungary, and Bulgaria. The three countries appear dependent on the EU's support. In particular, Bucharest and Budapest have been included as recipient countries in the 'Vienna Initiative', launched at the height of the financial crisis to prevent large-scale and uncoordinated bank failures in CEE. Bulgaria appears increasingly likely to need further European assistance in order to safeguard its financial stability.

As hypothesised (*H2b*), the two macro-clusters suggest that euro and non-euro member states frame and understand their national interests in different ways, especially when it comes to sharing the costs and the benefits of possible ways out of the crisis (that is, Eurobond or ESM). The sub-clusters highlight the presence of additional geo-territorial/economic cleavages within the macro-clusters. The effect of these cleavages seems residual if compared with euro membership. It is possible to identify: a southern sub-cluster, including Italy, Spain, and Romania; a CEE cluster, including Bulgaria, Slovenia, Estonia, and Lithuania; and a continental and northern cluster, including France, Germany, Austria, Belgium, and Finland. In the non-euro macro-cluster is the Scandinavian sub-cluster and the iron axis between British and Czech MEPs. Both are worth mentioning as they generally champion Euroscepticism.

Concluding Considerations

The primary objective of this study was to assess to what extent and in which direction the debate on the ongoing crisis affects the voting dynamics in the EP together with its distinctive government/opposition-like alignments. In this respect, competing partisan and nationally driven narratives are presented, debated, and tested in the empirical section of this study assuming the crisis-related votes to be: transnational; politically significant; nationally divisive; and ideologically divisive.

The comparison between the ECO and the CRISIS samples of votes confirmed the first set of hypotheses. Consequently, with economy-related votes, a burden-sharing tendency can be identified both within the main party groups and among them (*H1a*); the same cannot be said with respect to the crisis-related votes (*H2a*). The assessment of party groups' cohesion and coalition patterns shows a generalised decrease in voting coherence along partisan lines and an erosion of 'grand coalition' alignments in times of crisis (*H1b*). On the other hand, the impact of exogenous factors appears significant on the voting dynamics.

The cluster analysis based on the delegations' *Dvap* scores successfully categorised 26 delegations out of 27 in two macro-clusters, respectively consisting of five sub-clusters. The dendrogram in Figure 4 highlights a clear divide between euro and non-euro delegations, with very few exceptions.

Explanatory dimensions such as ideology appear residual. A more interest-based discourse is likely to be favoured. The emergence of a divide based on euro membership appears to reflect the diverging positions of two coalitions of actors with different interests and priorities. The same interest-based differences seem to be reflected in the five regional sub-clusters. These differences determine the acceptable costs and benefits presented by possible ways out of the crisis.

In conclusion, this comparative analysis provides a map to identify the dimensions of conflict in crisis-related debates affecting the government/opposition-like alignments and voting dynamics directly related to the parliamentarisation of the EP.

Funding

This research has been supported by the Estonian Research Council under grant projects ERMOS95.

Notes

1. Party groups in the sixth and seventh EP include Socialists and Democrats (S&D), the Alliance of Liberals and Democrats for Europe (ALDE), the European People's Party (EPP), European United Left–Nordic Green Left (GUE-NGL), Greens/EFA (G-EFA), Independence and Democracy (IND/DEM), Union for a Europe of Nations (UEN), Europe of Freedom and Democracy (EFD), and European Conservatives and Reformists (ECR).
2. See http://www.votewatch.eu/
3. According to article 160.1 of the Rules of Procedure of the European Parliament, 'the vote shall be taken by roll call if so requested in writing by a political group or at least 40 Members the evening before the vote unless the President sets a different deadline'. The RCVs represent only a portion of all the votes cast by the plenary. The RCVs are usually called by the party groups (Carrubba et al., 2002; Hix, 2002) either to show their position to the public or to embarrass other groups (Corbett, Shackleton, & Jacobs, 2000). While several scholars claim that the analyses based on RCVs might suffer from a structural selection bias (Carrubba et al., 2002; Rasmussen, 2008; Settembri, 2006), Hix (2002) maintains that 'RCVs cover a broad range of issues and do not appear to be called disproportionately by one EP party or another. Hence, without empirical evidence to prove that roll-call voting is systematically biased ... it is reasonable to assume that these votes should produce a fairly accurate picture of voting behaviour in the EP' (p. 693).
4. Although voting on resolutions does not seem to affect MEPs' collective behaviour in terms of cohesion and consensual/adversarial voting style (Carrubba et al., 2002), the relevance of the resolutions vis-à-vis other voting procedures has been proved by a number of studies (Carrubba et al., 2002). Motions for resolution typically outline the EP's stance on a particular issue and may call upon the EC to draft legislation in response. In particular, for issue areas that fall under the ordinary legislative procedure (as in the case of economic and monetary affairs), these calls may be important because again the EP will eventually be able to cast binding votes on the topic.
5. The votes computed in the cohesion test for the seventh EP include the 33 crisis-related RCVs (CRISIS sample) and the 1342 RCVs held in the current EP until our last observation held on 15 January 2013 (ALL sample). The ECO sample includes 125 votes on 'economic and monetary affairs', accounting for almost 10 per cent of the total. In the sixth EP the ALL sample includes 6149 votes, while the ECO sample includes 412 votes. Interestingly, the number of votes on 'economic and monetary affairs' has grown dramatically over the current term. No additional selection criterion has been applied at this stage.
6. Only bills with the modal voting option lower than or equal to 90 per cent have been included. Following the selection procedure, a total of 23 (out of 33) crisis-related RCVs have been included, accounting for almost 70 per cent of the universe of eligible RCVs.
7. There are two major methods of clustering, namely hierarchical clustering and k-means clustering. Here the former is preferred because this method allows the researcher to identify each phase of the process of segmentation, thereby delineating distinct subgroups (if any) within a broader cluster. Hierarchical clustering is represented by a two-dimensional diagram known as a dendrogram, which illustrates the fusions (upwards) or divisions (downwards) made at each successive stage of analysis and defined by the degrees of similarity.
8. Given the structurally high level of internal cohesion of the three mainstream parties, even a drop of a few percentage points in the groups' cohesion rate represents a significant indicator of decreasing internal voting coherence.
9. The Irish delegation was classified as not belonging to any cluster.

References

Attinà, F. (1990). The voting behaviour of the European Parliament members and the problem of the Europarties. *European Journal of Political Research, 18*(2), 557–579.

Braghiroli, S., & Smaldore, P. (2011, March). *One like no one? An assessment of the government–opposition dynamics in the EP*. Paper presented at the annual conference of the Italian Political Science Association, Palermo, Italy.

Carrubba, C. J., Clough, R., Montgomery, E., Murrah, L., Schambach, R., & Gabel, M. (2002). *Selection bias in the use of roll call votes to study legislative behavior* (Working Paper No. 11). London School of Economics and Political Science: European Parliament Research Group.

Chae, H. (2010). South Korean attitudes toward the ROK–U.S. alliance: Group analysis. *PS: Political Science & Politics, 43*(3), 493–500.

Corbett, R., Shackleton, M., & Jacobs, F. (2000). *The European Parliament* (4th ed.). London: Catermill.

Costa, O., & Magnette, P. (2003). The European Union as a consociation? A methodological assessment. *West European Politics, 26*(3), 1–18.

Elgström O., Bjurulf, B., & Johansson, J. (2001). Coalitions in European Union negotiations. *Scandinavian Political Studies, 24*(2), 111–128.

Faas, T. (2003). To defect or not to defect? National, institutional and party group pressures on MEPs and their consequences for party group cohesion in the European Parliament. *European Journal of Political Research, 42*(6), 841–866.

Fabbrini, S. (2005). Madison in Brussels: The EU and the US as compound democracies. *European Political Science, 4*(2), 188–198.

Hartigan, J. A. (1975). *Clustering algorithms (Probability & mathematical statistics)*. Chichester: John Wiley & Sons.

Helms, L. (2008). Parliamentary opposition and its alternatives in transnational regimes: The European Union in perspective. *The Journal of Legislative Studies, 14*(1/2), 212–235.

Hix, S. (1997). Executive selection in the European Union: Does the Commission president investiture procedure reduce the democratic deficit? *European Integration online Papers (EioP), 21*(1), digital version. Retrieved from http://eiop.or.at/eiop/texte/1997-021

Hix, S. (2002). Parliamentary behaviour with two principals: Preferences, parties, and voting in the European Parliament. *American Journal of Political Science, 46*(3), 688–698.

Hix, S. (2003, April). *The end of democracy in Europe? How the European Union (as currently designed) restricts political competition*. Paper presented at the conference Democracy in Europe, Harvard University.

Hix, S. (2005). *The political system of the European Union*. London: Palgrave.

Hix, S. (2011). *Voting in the 2009–2014 European Parliament: How do MEPs vote after Lisbon?* VoteWatch Third Report, VoteWatch Europe Papers.

Hix, S. (2013). *10 votes that shaped the 7th European Parliament*. VoteWatch Europe, Annual Report, VoteWatch Europe Papers.

Hix, S., & Lord, C. (1996). The making of a president: The European Parliament and the confirmation of Jacques Santer as president of the European Commission. *Government and Opposition, 31*(1), 62–76.

Hix, S., & Noury, A. (2009). After enlargement: Voting patterns in the Sixth European Parliament. *Legislative Studies Quarterly, 34*(2), 159–714.

Hix, S., Noury, A., & Roland, G. (2006). *Democratic politics in the European Parliament*. Cambridge: Cambridge University Press.

Kreppel, A. (2002). *The European Parliament and the supranational party system: A study of institutional development*. Cambridge: Cambridge University Press.

Lijphart, A. (1999). *Patterns of democracy*. New Haven, CT: Yale University Press.

Moravcsik, A. (1998). *The choice for Europe: Social purpose and state power from Messina to Maastricht*. Ithaca, NY: Cornell University Press.

Öhlén, M. (2013). *The eastward enlargement of European parties: Party adaptation in the light of EU-enlargement*. Örebro Studies in Political Science, 31. Örebro: Örebro University Press.

Rasmussen, A. (2008). Party soldiers in a non-partisan community? Party linkage in the European Parliament. *Journal of European Public Policy, 15*(8), 1164–1183.

Settembri, P. (2006, March). *Is the European Parliament competitive or consensual ... 'and why bother'?* Paper presented at the conference on the European Parliament and the European Political Space, London.

Spirling, A., & Quinn, K. (2010). Identifying intraparty voting blocs in the U.K. House of Commons. *Journal of the American Statistical Association, 105*(490), 447–457.

Taylor, P. (1991). The European Community and the state: Assumptions, theories and propositions. *Review of International Studies, 17*(2), 109–125.

Verney, S. (2009). Flaky fringe? Southern Europe facing the financial crisis. *South European Society and Politics, 14*(1), 1–6.

Voeten, E. (2005). *Legislator preferences, ideal points, and the spatial model in the European Parliament* (Working Paper No. 12). University of California Berkeley: Institute of Governmental Studies.

Von Hagen, J., Schuknechtd, L., & Wolswijk, G. (2009) *Government bond risk premiums in the EU revisited: The impact of the financial crisis*. CEPR Discussion Papers 7499.

Webb, P. (2008). The attitudinal assimilation of Europe by the Conservative Parliamentary Party. *British Politics, 4*(3), 427–444.

Zhong, S., & Ghosh, J. (2003). A unified framework for model-based clustering. *Journal of Machine Learning Research, 4*, 1001–1037.

Zimmer C., Schneider, G., & Dobbins, M. (2005). The contested council: Conflict dimensions of an intergovernmental EU institution. *Political Studies, 53*(2), 403–422.

Appendix: Crisis-related Votes Included in the Analysis

2080 Financial, economic and social crisis: measures and initiatives to be taken – Motion for a resolution: Paragraph 44/1, 06.07.2011

2076 Idem: Paragraph 13, 6 July 2011

2083 Idem: Paragraph 73, 6 July 2011

2081 Idem: Paragraph 44/2, 6 July 2011

2079 Idem: Paragraph 30, amendment 30, 6 July 2011

2077 Idem: Paragraph 29/1, 6 July 2011

2087 Idem: Paragraph 91, 6 July 2011

2090 Idem: Paragraph 107, 6 July 2011

2088 Idem: Paragraph 95, 6 July 2011

2082 Idem: Paragraph 57, 6 July 2011

2086 Idem: Paragraph 82, 6 July 2011

2084 Idem: Paragraph 76, 6 July 2011

2085 Idem: Paragraph 81, 6 July 2011

2078 Idem: Paragraph 29/2, 6 July 2011

2091 Idem: vote: (text as a whole), 6 July 2011

2089 Idem: After paragraph 99, amendment 18 = 36/2, 6 July 2011

1344 Motions for resolutions – Establishing a permanent crisis mechanism to safeguard the financial stability of the euro area – Motion for a resolution: Paragraph 20, 16 December 2010

1343 Idem: Paragraph 19, 16 December 2010

1342 Idem: After paragraph 15, amendment 2/2, 16 December 2010

1341 Idem: After paragraph 15, amendment 2/1, 16 December 2010

1340 Idem: After paragraph 14, amendment 12, 16 December 2010

1339 Idem: Paragraph 9/2, 16 December 2010

1346 Idem: vote: (text as a whole), 16 December 2010

1345 Idem: Recital C/2, 16 December 2010

1074 Financial, economic and social crisis: recommendations concerning the measures and initiatives to be taken – Motion for a resolution: After paragraph 181, amendment 3, 20 October 2010

1073 Idem: Paragraph 103, 20 October 2010

1070 Idem: Paragraph 83, 20 October 2010
1072 Idem: Paragraph 101, 20 October 2010
1076 Idem: vote: (text as a whole), 20 October 2010
1075 Idem: Paragraph 190, 20 October 2010
1071 Idem: Paragraph 92, 20 October 2010
1069 Idem: Paragraph 77, 20 October 2010
1068 Idem: Paragraph 68, 20 October 2010
2522 Motions for resolutions – Feasibility of introducing stability bonds – Motion for a resolution: vote: (text as a whole), 15 February 2012

Conclusions: Great Recession, Great Cooperation?

ELISABETTA DE GIORGI and CATHERINE MOURY

Contributions to this study clearly support our initial hypotheses. It is observed, as expected, that the economic crisis has considerably decreased consensual behaviour in parliament. However, the nature of parties constitutes a crucial variable in order to explain the conduct of the opposition in the legislative arena better: since the outbreak of the crisis, radical parties have turned even more adversarial than before; whereas mainstream parties – who want to appear as a credible alternative to the government in office – have drifted towards more cooperative behaviour. Given the growing influence of the European Union on the legislation approved in response to the crisis, it was also expected (and demonstrated) that the traditionally pro-European parties would be more likely to cooperate on socio-economic issues than Eurosceptic parties. Finally, it has also been shown that timing also plays an important role in the opposition's decision either to support or to oppose the government: with opposition parties more inclined to contest the government's proposals when their chances of getting into power are higher, and vice versa.

In national legislatures, MPs from the opposition are often torn between the desire to dissent from the government in order to present themselves to the electorate as an attractive alternative, and the will to collaborate with the incumbents so as to get a chance to influence the content of legislation. In normal times, the latter prevails: opposition parties often cooperate with the majority. In the European Parliament (EP), there is clearly a similar trend towards cooperation, and a *grand coalition* composed of the three major parties is the most frequent combination of votes. Since the outbreak of the economic crisis, however, conflicting pressures on opposition MPs both to cooperate and to distance themselves from the governments in office have intensified considerably. The opposition has had to choose between cooperating with the majority for the nation's sake in order to influence the direction of far-reaching socio-economic changes, and going against an already fragile government so as possibly to get into power itself. For the members of the EP (MEPs) similar pressures can be observed: party groups have incentives to cooperate with each other in order to increase the EP's influence at a time when decisions are often taken outside the EU institutional structure; but they also have more reasons than before to split across ideological and territorial lines. This issue has explored how the opposition parties in southern European legislatures and political parties in the EP responded to this dilemma.

In the Introduction to this issue, we made three broad assumptions with regard to this question. First, we hypothesised a decrease in the level of consensus in parliament in the aftermath of the crisis. This was so because much of the legislation presented in parliament in past years is salient and deals with economic and social aspects: both characteristics that have been proved to favour dissension. Our second hypothesis assumed a different legislative behaviour in accordance with the type of party. We posited that the mainstream parties, which usually alternate in government and opposition, are more likely to be led by a sense of responsibility and consequently vote for (or let pass) measures that, no matter how unpopular, could help save the country from the worst effects of the crisis. Moreover, as most of the socio-economic policy proposals follow the requirements of the European Commission (EC) – in some cases, also in collaboration with the European Central Bank (ECB) and the International Monetary Fund (IMF) – we also expected parties' attitudes towards European integration to be an important factor in explaining their collaboration with the government (or lack thereof). One last hypothesis was related to the shift in time, within the national contexts. Austerity measures are by their nature unpopular, as is the government that has to implement them. Therefore, we posited that, following the start of a financial crisis, the opposition behaves in a more conflictual way when the government's incumbency is at risk, for instance when it lacks a majority of seats in parliament or its popularity declines dramatically, and in a less conflictual way when it is not, that being when elections have just been held or technocratic governments, rather than true political competitors, are in charge.

Contributions to this issue clearly support our hypotheses and give additional crucial insights into the behaviour of the opposition parties in times of crisis. First, we observe that the crisis has led to a considerable decrease in the consensual behaviour in parliament. The works on Spain and Portugal testify to a significant decline of favourable votes or abstentions from the opposition benches. The main reason for this decline, as we posited, is the rising number of socio-economic and salient policies voted on in parliament. In Italy and Greece, the crisis has not only led to more adversarial behaviour of the opposition, but also produced visible dissension within the party (or coalition of parties) supporting the government. Marangoni and Verzichelli illustrate how the Monti government was obliged to ask for a vote of confidence in parliament on many occasions to ensure passage of its legislation, and was forced to resign a few months before the end of its term when the main centre-right party, People of Freedom Party (PDL) – which had been part of the majority until that time – decided to withdraw its support of the executive. And after the 2013 general election, the mutual veto of the main parties blocked the formation of a new executive for two whole months. In the contribution on Greece, Gemenis and Nezi remind us that the Panhellenic Socialist Party was the only party to support both the first bailout package and the midterm plan, while Prime Minister Papandreou was often challenged by his own MPs. Consensus politics emerged only during the talks for the coalition government, but these only started after the EU put pressure on the Greek political parties, and did not last long. The cases of Italy and Greece also show us another indirect impact of the crisis on parliamentary dynamics: the sudden polarisation and fragmentation of the party system. In Italy, a new political force – the Five Star Movement – led by the famous blogger Beppe Grillo, made a spectacular entrance into parliament in February 2013 when it got more than 25 per cent of votes. In Greece, an even more important fragmentation of the party system was observed. The 2012 elections were extremely volatile and led to a doubling of the effective number of parties in parliament (from two to four). In the EP, Braghiroli finally observed a fall in consensus in crisis-related votes (as compared with all votes and all economic votes), putting members and non-members of the eurozone and those from southern and central eastern Europe and continental and northern Europe against each other.

Our second hypothesis derives from the existing literature asserting that the nature of parties constitutes a crucial variable explaining the behaviour of the opposition in parliament. In particular, we expected radical parties to be even more adversarial following the outbreak of the crisis, and mainstream parties – which usually want to appear to the electorate to be a credible alternative to the government in office – to drift towards cooperation. Given the growing influence of the EU on the legislation approved in response to the crisis, we also expected the traditionally pro-European parties to be more likely to cooperate on those measures than Eurosceptic parties. This hypothesis was clearly supported by our case studies as well. In Portugal, in particular, both the qualitative and quantitative analyses carried out by De Giorgi, Moury, and Ruivo demonstrate how the net effect of the crisis varies strongly across parties. While mainstream and traditionally pro-European parties (first the Social Democrats in opposition and then the Socialists) are less adversarial than they would be in normal times, the exact opposite is true for the Communists (PCP) and Greens (PEV), two radical left and Eurosceptic parties. Exactly as we expected, the Conservative CDS-PP – which is less pro-European than the other mainstream parties – appeared less cooperative. On the other hand, the other radical left party (BE) – which is less Eurosceptic than PCP and PEV – was found to be less controversial than its radical left counterpart.

Similarly, Marangoni and Verzichelli observe a clear association in the Italian case between a 'core European' party family and the loyalty to the proposals of the Monti government. Alternatively, they note that the Eurosceptic parties, notably the Northern League, adopted a less cooperative stance on the socio-economic legislation proposed by the EU institutions. In Spain, where none of the parties could be qualified as Eurosceptic, this hypothesis is harder to test. However, Chaqués-Bonafont, Muñoz Márquez, and Palau observe that the radical left party IU, which had never governed and had been more critical than its counterparts towards the Maastricht and Constitutional treaties, is the parliamentary group that opposes the most EU-related legislation. In Greece, the pro/anti-European dimension is proved not only to affect the voting behaviour of opposition parties, but also to be a very powerful explanatory factor for understanding the implosion of the party system. Gemenis and Nezi demonstrate how the economic crisis has increased the importance of European integration to the national party system; and how this dimension accounts for many of the fissures and shifts witnessed between 2010 and 2012. Another indicator of the significance of the EU was evident during the talks for the coalition agreement, which started only after the EU put pressure on the political parties to collaborate with each other so that Greece could enact an emergency funding package. Finally, in the EP, Braghiroli has shown how the decline of consensus in crisis-related votes is much more important for the EFD (the populist radical right group) and GUE (the extreme left) than for the other party families.

Finally, according to our third hypothesis, we expected that timing would play a key role in the opposition's decision either to support or to contest the government, with parties more inclined to oppose when their chances to get into power increase, and vice versa. This is clearly demonstrated in our analyses on Spain and Portugal. In Portugal, De Giorgi, Moury and Ruivo show how both the PSD and the PS changed their voting behaviour from cooperative to conflictual when the electorate's voting intentions moved in their favour. Similarly, statistical regression in the Spanish contribution illustrates that the opposition behaves less consensually when the popularity of the government decreases. In Greece, opportunistic behaviour also prevailed: at times of high volatility, none of the opposition parties agreed to support the first bailout package or the midterm plan. Consensus politics emerged only during the talks for the coalition government, but stopped as soon as the political actors who supported the government discovered the electoral costs of their collaboration. In Italy, after Silvio Berlusconi's resignation in November 2011, a coalition formed by the centre-left PD and centre-right PDL decided to support the new technocratic government led by Mario Monti, together with some minor moderate parties from the centre. But, as noted above, the support for the government was always at risk: long negotiations and votes of confidence were often required in order to assure the passage of relevant legislation given the low level of party cohesiveness, notably within the centre-right. What is more, the PDL decided to withdraw strategically its support of the executive at the end of 2012, probably in view of the approaching general election. In sum, all contributions to this issue show that, although a sense of responsibility and pro-European attitudes might induce mainstream parties to cooperate with the government for the country's sake, party self-interest would always prevail eventually.

Thus, we do observe marked similarities across our cases regarding the impact of the economic crisis on the legislative behaviour of political actors. In all four cases, the crisis lowered the level of consensus. While mainstream parties are more likely to act responsibly – unless their chances to get into power increase significantly – radical parties clearly have behaved in a more adversarial way since the beginning of the crisis. The inclusion of the EP in this study demonstrates how hypotheses based on the literature on national legislatures also apply to the supranational context.

We did, however, observe fundamental differences across countries as well. In the course of 2011, the prime minister of each of the four countries under analysis resigned and the government was replaced. But this outcome was reached in two different ways: through the call for new elections and the victory of the parties that were previously in opposition in Portugal and Spain; and through the formation of a new parliamentary majority supporting the government without going to the polls in Greece and Italy. Moreover, the crisis led to an overhaul of the party system in the latter two cases. On the one hand, Italy saw the return of technical governments as in the 1990s and then the rise of anti-party sentiment, which brought success to the Five Star Movement. In Greece, the new executive led by Papademos lasted only a few months and was followed by two general elections in rapid succession (in May and June 2012). Moreover, the party system was completely split on the grounds of a latent pro-integration dimension. By contrast, Portugal and Spain seem to have reached greater political stability following the elections of 2011. Thus, the stability of the electoral and party system – rather than the seriousness of the crisis or the external interventions – seems to be a fundamental factor in explaining the intensity of the impact of the crisis on parliamentary dynamics.

In the present issue, we have focused exclusively on the opposition in parliament. However, alternative strategies of dissent obviously exist. Southern European countries actually put in place a variety of alternative strategies outside parliament. In Italy, the relative ease with which the government managed to pass the extremely ambitious reforms is striking: protests had been quite modest, probably due to the fact that the technocratic government was perceived by public opinion as the only solution to prevent economic collapse and a consequent bailout. The same could be said for Portugal, where the population has been relatively quiet despite very harsh measures (with the exception of the demonstration of September 2012, which mobilised around 1.5 million people in several cities). But many alternative strategies emerged in Greece and Spain: such as referendums, street demonstrations and occupation of town squares. The movement of the so-called *Indignados*, for instance, was born spontaneously in Spain but then spread all over Europe. This was certainly one further consequence of the strong intervention of international external actors in the economic and political situation of the nation states and in the decisions taken by national governments. The role of parliament and, above all, of the opposition parties, was perceived as very limited, and citizens – as well as some of the opposition parties themselves, notably the more radical ones – opted for arenas other than parliament and different strategies in order to pursue their objectives. This only demonstrates more clearly that opposition MPs have no easy answer when they have to choose between collaborating with, or opposing, the government.

Index